Beyond
Twilight

Explore the Hidden World of the Vampires

This edition published in 2010 by Bounty Books,
a division of Octopus Publishing Group Ltd
Endeavour House,
189 Shaftesbury Avenue,
London WC2H 8JY

An Hachette UK Company
www.hachette.co.uk

ISBN: 978-0-753719-27-5

A CIP catalogue record for this book is available from the
British Library

Printed and bound in China

Beyond Twilight

Explore the Hidden World of the Vampires

MANUELA DUNN-MASCETTI

Bounty
Books

Contents

Introduction

The Doors to Darkness

The figure of the vampire, a creature clad in darkness and legend, who awakens at night and drinks the life-force of his victims in order to replenish his own, has haunted man's imagination for centuries. There is enough material in the legends, hear-says, witness accounts and true facts reported over the centuries to give fuel to a compulsive fascination with the horror of the walking dead.

The fear of the vampire does not arise only from fantasy, but often from substantial and documented reports. Europe, especially its eastern borders, was at times plagued by hordes of vampires who literally bled the population of medieval villages to death. The more precise investigations of science were summoned by local priests or the lords of the manor in attempts to put an end to the horrors perpetuated at night in their districts. Visiting scientists discovered that vampires had an extensive history and a clear lineage of their own and were not, as was previously thought, simply a local phenomenon. Their origins could in fact be traced to ancient Egyptian times when the cult and worship of the dead was ritually represented by ceremonies in which the acolytes revered a divinity that looked like a dark bird. This sinister bird represented the flight of the soul at the moment of death and its journey into the world of shadows. The dead, who were 'alive' in their own world, occasionally came to plague the inhabitants of the world of light and some-times even took them back into the unknown, stealing their lives away.

As Austrian troops took possession of the lands that lie near the eastern borders of Europe, parts of Serbia and Wallachia, the occupying forces began to notice and file reports on a peculiar local practice. The local population would exhume bodies in order to 'kill' them. Literate outsiders began to attend such exhumations and write reports on what they saw. These witness accounts, perhaps sometimes distorted by fertile imaginations, filtered through into Austria, Germany, France and England. The rest of Europe thus became aware of practices that were by no means of recent origin, but had simply been provided, for the first time, with effective 'publicity' of 'the strange goings-on in Transylvania.' The Slavic vampire, or *upir* as it was often called, found echo in similar creatures in other parts of Europe who were referred to in their own cultures by entirely different names.

The fact that these phenomena were restricted not only to a small, barbaric area, but were also found everywhere else, gave credence to the vampire as we know him today. European scholars found cases of 'undead' in far-off cultures such as China, Indonesia and the Philippines. It seemed that vampires existed everywhere, and in a variety of cultures. The vampires were dead people who, having died before their time, not only refused to remain dead, but returned to bring death to their friends and neighbours.

Victorian vampirism was given a complex tone of sexual innuendo and baroque elegance by the literature of the time.

Death brings death, a fond and most ancient belief and the foundation of a host of complex and undeniable instincts. Modern man has long lost touch with his deeper intuitions, those dark, often emotional wells of understanding that are not associated with reason. The vampire, ancient and modern, is truly born from these regions of the unconscious with small but significant remnants surfacing to bring us intensely tantalizing hints, keeping our interest without ever providing the whole truth.

This book has grown from these dark rumours and legends, gathered together over thousands of years, recorded in stories, accounts and encounters that tell of the black angels that stalk the world, refusing to die. Information for the researcher is diffuse and secretive, often confusing, and tends to cast an unexpected sense of uncertainty over those who delve. Nothing precise can be delineated, nothing which gives the researcher reason to rationalize, only a deep sense of doubt, arguments with loved ones, premonitions of danger, dreams of fleeing or attacking monsters and the tendency to live under a kind of shadow, the shadow that the vampire displays when he opens his cape for his victim to enter.

Thus the reader enters this book with a warning, for these pages contain the essence of the Princes of Darkness, the sense being that dust may lie upon the surfaces, that the book was taken from the library of Count Dracula himself, the arch collector, ultimately elegant and entirely dangerous. Look out for blood hidden with stealth between the lines of the legends – fact or fiction, who knows the difference? Perhaps there is none in this reality and to enjoy this book is to enter just that reality.

Chapter 1

The Anatomy of a Vampire

Is it a human being, and therefore a 'he' or a 'she', or truly an 'it', a monstrously evil and hideously ugly creature which happens to bear human form? This dilemma between its recognizably human form and the possibility of its deterioration into a monstrous appearance is in fact one of the keys to understanding the popularization of vampires, both in the past centuries and today. The vampire's form, though we can see it to be human, is also available in a grotesquely distorted version, giving us the true horror of the contrast between soft human flesh and rotting death.

The physical features are repulsive: long nails that curve like claws; skin showing deathly pallor, except when flushed after feeding; eyes often described as dead but nevertheless possessing a hypnotic stare; and rat-like fangs prepared for attack. The vampire is also psychologically repulsive: he is evil, devoid of any moral code; he stands outside and therefore threatens all normal society; he drinks blood; he kills without mercy; and, worse of all, he is capable of the final and most inhuman of acts, transforming his victims into equally horrific creatures, a unilateral decision that no mere human under his power is strong enough to prevent.

The result of such transformation is ostensibly an ordinary man or woman who, through very strange rituals involving the exchange of blood, is endowed with immortality. But the quality of the vampire's immortality is tinged with the punishment that belongs to he who defies natural law. Vampires live on the other side; they are the dead who have chosen to live among the living, rather than ascend or descend to those places where all souls must rest before undertaking another life's journey. Their world is cold, dark and lonely. The hand of death guides their every action, and it is a yoke they must bear forever. As we will see, it has long been the living human's fondest desire to prevent the occurrence of a returning soul, in order to pave the way for eternal rest for the dead. Even the headstones we see in our local cemeteries everywhere in the world were originally intended simply to prevent the dead from sitting up in their graves!

For the vampire must kill, his duty is to bring evil to the communities of fair men, for he is the servant of she who is insatiable, Mistress Death. Vampires thus plague lost villages in the mountains or in marshlands, they roam around the darkness of forests, they take residence in abandoned castles, and nowadays their presence is felt even in harbours, building sites and other lonely corners of the modern metropolis.

But mankind has built up quite a dossier of information and material surrounding the appearance of the vampire and his somewhat disgusting habits. This process of collecting and gathering information was not simply motivated by fascination, but was intended to aid future sufferers of vampiric activity in their quest to rid themselves of this horrible plague. Recognizing the problem is half way to solving it.

There is, therefore, available to us ordinary mortals a wealth of information on how to recognize a vampire. Some characteristics have become better known than others, presumably through greater use. For example, the fact that vampires fear the sun, crucifixes and garlic; they cannot cross water; they sleep in coffins and prefer young virgins as their victims; they must always carry a little of their native soil wherever they go; and they must always have an evil assistant to do their dirty work by day.

Other facts may be less familiar but should still be noted, for often the lesser-known is the greater in importance. Vampires also have the reputation of conniving secrecy concerning their own weaknesses. There are, for example, both male and female vampires; there are vampires who are visible and others who can change their shape at will; there are vampires who do not suck blood from their victims at all. Instead, they prefer to steal things that are perhaps more valuable to a human being, such as youth, hope and love.

It may be that we find the vampire so compelling precisely because he is so repellent. He works so powerfully on our imaginations because he represents such a distortion of human nature, a reversal of everything normal. This is one of the weapons that the vampire uses to invite his victims to meet death and the process of transformation that will make them like him. He catches our imaginations and lures us towards a path of despair that looks and feels deceptively attractive. This is his greatest skill although, as we shall learn, he has many others too.

It is for this very reason that men and women before us wrote accounts of fearsome and strange encounters with vampires. To warn us of the dangers, to give us clues that will counteract the powerful force of vampire seductions. The following pages describe exactly the physical nature of vampires as found in those accounts. The research has been gathered from all corners of the earth, across centuries, to give the reader the widest spectrum so that he may be warned, and thus saved.

Grave Discoveries

A long time before vampires filled the pages of romantic horror stories, such as Bram Stoker's *Dracula,* and became so popular as to be portrayed in both fiction and movies, they are said to have plagued rural villages in those lost corners of eastern Europe such as the provinces of Hungary, Romania and Transylvania. The popular depiction of a vampire, the one that is most familiar to us, is of a tall, very thin, aristocratic man. He is dressed in a black suit and a long, enveloping black cape. As a concession to his origins, the outfit of the classic vampire may be a little dusty and worn-looking, having seen better days, but he is essentially an elegant character who, at first glance, we might not discard out of hand. However, on slightly closer examination we find that his irksome smile reveals protuberant, exaggeratedly long, and extremely sharp canine teeth. His breath is foul; his nails long and crooked like the talons of a beast; his complexion so pale he looks as if he has just arisen from the grave.

But is this how the vampires that are said to have haunted villages really looked? Not at all. In fact, for the sake of the watchful, it is now important to look at a very different form of vampire from our rather grotesque but essentially elegant movie character, one that stalked the country lanes and fields of the distant past – a creature that may still be present in our darker regions. The following eyewitness reports give us the very best sources of proof.

Eyewitness Account I: Peter Plogojowitz

The story of Peter Plogojowitz dates back to 1725 and was witnessed by German military officials stationed in the village of Kisilova, in the Rahm District, now Slavia. Kisilova was actually in Serbia although, because of the confused political situation of the time, it has often been reported as being part of Hungary.

Our subject, Peter Plogojowitz, had died ten weeks past. He had been buried according to the Raetzian custom, a local religious ritual of the time. It was revealed that in his village, during a period of a week, nine people, both old and young, had also died after suffering a 24-hour illness. Each of them had publicly declared, "that while they were yet alive, but on their death-bed, the above mentioned Plogojowitz, who had died ten weeks earlier, had come to them in their sleep, laid himself on them, and throttled them, so that they would have to give up the ghost."

Those who heard these reports were naturally very distressed by them, and their belief in the authenticity of them was strengthened even more by the fact that Peter Plogojowitz's wife, after saying that her husband had come to her and demanded his *opanki*, or shoes, had left the village of Kisilova.

And since with such people (which they call vampires) various are to be seen that is, the body undecomposed, the skin, hair, beard and nails growing, the subjects resolved unanimously to open the grave of Peter Plogojowitz and to see if such above-mentioned signs were really to be found on him. To this end they came here to me and, telling of these events, asked me and the local Pope, or parish priest, to be present at the viewing. And although I at first disapproved, telling them that the praise-worthy administration should first be dutifully and humbly informed, and its exalted opinion about this should be heard, they did not want to accommodate themselves to this at all, but rather gave this short answer: I could do what I wanted, but if I did not accord them the viewing and the legal recognition to deal with the body according to their custom, they would have to leave house and home, because by the time a gracious resolu-

tion was received from Belgrade, perhaps the entire village (and this was already supposed to have happened in Turkish times) could be destroyed by such an evil spirit, and they did not want to wait for this.

The narrator goes on to say that,

Since I could not hold these people from the resolution they had made, either with good words or with threats, I went to the village of Kisilova, taking along the Gradisk Pope, and viewed the body of Peter Plogojowitz, just exhumed, finding, in accordance with thorough truthfulness, that first of all I did not detect the slightest odour that is otherwise characteristic of the dead, and the body, except for the nose, which was somewhat fallen away, was completely fresh. The hair and beard, even the nails, of which the old ones had fallen away, had grown on him; the old skin, which was somewhat whitish, had peeled away, and a new one had emerged from it. The face, hands and feet and the whole body were so constituted, that they could not have been more complete in his lifetime. Not without astonishment, I saw some fresh blood in his mouth, which, according to the common observation, he had sucked from the people killed by him. In short, all the indications were present that such people (as remarked above) are said to have. After both the Pope and I had seen this spectacle, while people grew more outraged than distressed, all the subjects, with great speed, sharpened a stake in order to pierce the corpse of the deceased with it – and put this at his heart, whereupon, as he was pierced, not only did much blood, completely fresh, flow also through his ears and mouth, but still other wild signs (which I pass by out of high respect) took place. Finally, according to their usual practice, they burned the often-mentioned body, in hic casu, to ashes of which I inform the most laudable Administration, and at the same time would like to request, obediently and humbly, that if a mistake was made in this matter, such is to be attributed not to me but to the rabble, who were beside themselves with fear.

Each of the investigative accounts concerning the instance of vampires that were documented during the medieval period of European history had to be sealed by either a local official or a doctor. The seals above have been reproduced from actual seals found on the reports on these pages.

This lengthy account, written in the style characteristic of bureaucratic eastern Europe of the eighteenth century, reveals that the vampire, Peter Plogojowitz, was an ordinary peasant of the village of Kisilova. Unfortunately, the account does not tell us anything about his personality or physical characteristics before his death, but it is quite clear from the description that he was not from aristocratic stock, nor was he wearing a long black cape and a black tuxedo in his coffin, hardly details that would have been overlooked. The account illustrates quite clearly the difference, at least in appearance, between the fictional and the folkloric vampire. The former, as we have already described, is elegant, aristocratic and eccentric, with the grotesque aspect of his nature only visible beneath the outer glamour at second glance. The latter is perhaps even more treacherous, for he is just like you and me, indistinguishable from the millions of people who inhabit the earth. It seems important, therefore, to proceed to examine very carefully the characteristics of Peter Plogojowitz as described, so that we may become familiar with the vampire species in all its potential forms. We can start by examining, through careful study of the above report, some classic signs of vampirism.

1. It might seem, on close examination of the report, that vampirism occurs as an epidemic. Evidence of this arises from the fact that first Peter Plogo- jowitz died and then, within the space of a week, nine other people, both old and young, also died, in each case from a sudden 24-hour illness. Peter Plogojowitz is held responsible for the deaths of the other people, just as a victim of an epidemic illness, such as the plague, might have been held responsible for the deaths of his fellow villagers. In light of modern medi- cine we might dismiss such an idea right away, but maybe this is the mistake of rational man always using concrete evidence when mystery is lurking just beneath the surface, eating away at certainty. To the peasant, always aware of magic, vampirism was an epidemic. One vampire caused another vampire, who in turn caused a third, and so on. If they didn't move fast to rid themselves of this plague, then all their neighbours and friends would go the same way, and the village would soon spread its infection to the town, to the country, and eventually the world would be populated by

the walking dead. This must have been the ultimate fear of those subjected to such experiences as that of Peter Plogojowitz. This fear still exists in the mind and memory of mankind, evidenced by short stories such as *Place of Meeting* by Charles Beaumont (1953) and still more recent stories and movies depicting the presence of the living dead in various forms.

2. The vampire leaves his grave at night, appears before his victims and either sucks blood or strangles them. This kind of vampire is known to experts as the ambulatory type and is the most common vampire of all.

3. The body is said to be 'completely fresh': the nose has fallen in, but the hair, beard and nails have grown and new skin has formed under the old. This is an important characteristic of vampires: they do not appear dead when exhumed. On the contrary, they show signs of rejuvenation.

4. The body has no foul odour. But this may not necessarily be typical of vampires. An eighteenth-century ecclesiast, Don Calmet, observed that "when they (vampires) have been taken out of the ground, they have appeared red, with their limbs supple and pliable, without worms or decay; but not without great stench." The stench of the body is an important aspect of the nexus between vampirism and the plague. As we said before, in European folklore vampires cause epidemics. Foul smells were commonly associated with disease, even with the cause of disease. It was not unreasonable to imagine that as corpses smelled bad, bad smells must be a cause of disease and death. In order to combat such smells, strong-smelling substances such as aromatic softwoods, juniper and ash were used. Vampirism, therefore, was believed to be catching.

5. We should note perhaps the strongest evidence of Peter Plogojowitz's vampiric state was the fresh blood of his victims still trickling from his mouth. Unless this was somehow planted there, it would seem hard to deny as a piece of clear proof. How many corpses manage to retain uncongealed blood? In addition, his own blood was still fresh and uncongealed, thus also condemning him as a vampire.

6. We learn that when the villagers stake the vampire, he bleeds profusely after several weeks in the grave. The 'wild signs' of which the author spares us details probably implies that the corpse's penis was erect. The vampire

is a sexual creature, and his sexuality is obsessive. In Yugoslavian legends, for example, when the vampire is not sucking blood, he is apt to wear out his widow with his attentions, so that she too wastes away, much like his other victims. This also raises the question of whether a vampire's activities are restricted to blood sucking, or whether his young female victims may also suffer rape.

We can draw the conclusion that Peter Plogojowitz was the first person in his village to catch a genuine case of vampirism and, by infecting others with it, made a place for himself in history.

We can use this first example to begin a list of vampire characteristics:

1. The power to create a kind of epidemic of blood lust among chosen individuals, both male and female.
2. Vampires appear 'undead' in the grave: the skin is fresh and there is no evident decomposition; fresh blood still flows in their veins.
3. There appears to be evidence that the vampire also retains a strong sexual appetite and that this vigour exists even in the grave.

Eyewitness Account II: *Visum et Repertum*

The following report is perhaps the most notable instance of vampirism in which a whole village is affected. The case was so serious that it finally attracted the attention of the authorities and led to the report being known to history as *Visum et Repertum* (Seen and Discovered). The story is mainly associated with a man named Arnod Paole who died as the result of a fall from a haywagon. His death would no doubt have gone unnoticed had it not been for the fact that he was subsequently exhumed, staked and burned. The report, made some time after the event, is a curious and fascinating document.

VISUM ET REPERTUM

After it had been reported that in the village of Medvegia the so-called vampires had killed some people by sucking their blood. I was, by high decree of a local Honourable Supreme Command, sent there to investigate the matter thoroughly, along with officers detailed for that purpose and two subordinate medical officers, and therefore carried out and heard the present inquiry in the company of the captain of the Stallath Company of haiduks (a type of soldier), Gorschiz Hadnack, the bariactar (standard-bearer) and the oldest haiduk of the village, as follows: who unanimously recount that about five years ago a local haiduk by the name of Arnod Paole broke his neck in a fall from a haywagon. This man had during his lifetime often revealed that, near Gossowa in Turkish Serbia, he had been troubled by a vampire, wherefore he had eaten from the earth of the vampire's grave and had smeared himself with the vampire's blood, in order to be free from the vexation he had suffered. In 20 or 30 days after his death, some people complained that they were being bothered by this same Arnod Paole; and in fact four people were killed by him. In order to end this evil, they dug up this Arnod Paole 40 days after his death, this on the advice of their hadnack (soldier), who had been present at such events before; and they found that he was quite complete and undecayed, and that fresh blood had flowed from his eyes, nose, mouth and ears; that the shirt, the covering and the coffin were completely bloody; that the old nails on his hands and feet, along with the skin, had fallen off, and that new ones had grown; and since they saw from this that he

The angels that guard over the
dead in our graveyards often take
on the atmosphere of the
darkness they protect us from.

Williams Blake's rendition of tragic loss in the eighteenth century.

was a true vampire, they drove a stake through his heart, according to their custom, whereby he gave an audible groan and bled copiously. Thereupon they burned the body the same day to ashes and threw these into the grave. These people say further that all those who were tormented and killed by the vampire must themselves become vampires. Therefore they disinterred the above-mentioned four people in the same way. Then they also add that this Arnod Paole attacked not only the people but also the cattle, and sucked out their blood. And since the people used the flesh of such cattle, it appears that some vampires are again present here, in as much as, in a period of three months, 17 young and old people died, among them some who, with no previous illness, died in two or at the most three days. In addition, the haiduk Jowiza reports that his step-daughter, by name of Stanacka, lay down to sleep 15 days ago, fresh and healthy, but at midnight she started up out of her sleep with a terrible cry, fearful and trembling, and complained that she had been throttled by the son of a haiduk by the name of Milloe, who had died nine weeks earlier, whereupon she had experienced a great pain in the chest and became worse hour by hour, until finally she died on the third day. At this we went the same afternoon to the graveyard, along with the often-mentioned oldest haiduks of the village, in order to cause the suspicious graves to be opened and to examine the bodies in them, whereby, after all of them had been dissected, there was found:

1. *A woman by the name of Stana, 20 years old, who had died in childbirth two months ago, after a three-day illness, and who had herself said, before her death, that she had painted herself with the blood of a vampire, where-fore both she and her child, which had died right after birth and because of a careless burial had been half eaten by the dogs, must also become vampires. She was quite complete and undecayed. After the opening of the body there was found in the cavitate pectoris a quantity of fresh extravascular blood. The vasa (vessels) of the arteriae and venae, like the ventriculis ortis, were not, as is usual, filled with coagulated blood, and the whole viscera, that is, the pulmo (lung), hepar (liver), stomachus, lien (spleen) et intestina were quite fresh as they would be in a healthy person. The uterus was however quite enlarged and very inflamed externally, for the placenta*

and lochia had remained in place, wherefore the same was in complete putredine. The skin on her hands and feet, along with the old nails, fell away on their own, but on the other hand completely new nails were evident, along with a fresh and vivid skin.

2. There was a woman by the name of Miliza (60 years old), who had died after a three-month sickness and had been buried 90-some days earlier. In the chest much liquid blood was found, and the other viscera were, like those mentioned before, in a good condition. During her dissection, all the haiduks who were standing around marvelled greatly at her plumpness and perfect body, uniformly stating that they had known the woman well, from her youth, and that she had, throughout her life, looked and been very lean and dried up, and they emphasized that she had come to this surprising plumpness in the grave. They also said that it was she who started the vampires this time, because she had eaten of the flesh of those sheep that had been killed by the previous vampires.

3. There was an eight-day-old child which had lain in the grave for 90 days and was similarly in a condition of vampirism.

4. The son of a haiduk, 16 years old, was dug up, having lain in the earth for nine weeks after he had died from a three-day illness, and was found like the other vampires.

5. Joachim, also the son of a haiduk, 17 years old, had died after a three-day illness. He had been buried eight weeks and four days and, on being dissected, was found in similar condition.

6. A woman by the name of Ruscha who had died after a ten-day illness and had been buried six weeks previous, in whom there was much fresh blood not only in the chest but also in fundo ventriculi. The same showed itself in her child, which was 18 days old and had died five weeks previously.

7. No less did a girl ten years of age, who had died two months previously, find herself in the above-mentioned condition, quite complete and undecayed, and had much fresh blood in her chest.

8. They caused the wife of the Hadnack to be dug up, along with her child. She had died seven weeks before, her child who was eight weeks old 21 days previously. Both mother and child were completely decomposed,

This picture brings to mind the words of the French philosopher Jacques Lacan – "The mirror might reflect a little longer returning an image to its owner."

    although the earth and grave were like those of the vampires lying nearby.

9. *A servant of the local corporal of the haiduks, by the name of Rhade, 23 years old, died after a three-month-long illness, and after a five-week burial was found completely decomposed.*

10. *The wife of the local bariactar, along with her child, having died five weeks previously, were also completely decomposed.*

11. *With Stanche, a local haiduk, 60 years old, who had died six weeks ago, I noticed a profuse liquid blood, like the others, in the chest and stomach. The entire body was in the oft-named condition of vampirism.*

12. *Milloe, a haiduk, 25 years old, who had lain for six weeks in the earth, also was found in the condition of vampirism mentioned.*

13. *Stanoika, the wife of a haiduk, 20 years old, died after a three-day illness and had been buried 18 days previously. In the dissection I found that she was in her countenance quite red and of a vivid colour, and, as was mentioned above, she had been throttled, at midnight, by Milloe, the son of the haiduk, and there was also to be seen, on the right side under the ear, a bloodshot blue mark, the length of a finger. As she was being taken out of the grave, a quantity of fresh blood flowed from her nose. With the dissection I found, as mentioned often already, a regular fragrant fresh bleeding, not only in the chest cavity, but also in* ventriculo cordis. *All the viscera found themselves in a completely good and healthy condition. The hypodermis of the entire body, along with the fresh nails of hands and feet, was as though completely fresh. After the examination had taken place, the heads of the vampires were cut off by the local gypsies and burned along with the bodies, and then the ashes were thrown into the river Morava. The decomposed bodies, however, were laid back into their own graves.*

Such an account could more easily have been written within the pages of a work of horror fiction. But this and many more such reports, signed and witnessed by local and even city officials and doctors, have formed the very real basis for belief in vampirism. These events, even though well-hidden within the yellowing pages of history books, are true as far as any historic event can be proven. They also created a very real and horrific fascination for the cultured ear of the romantic spirit that pervaded Europe at the time. It is easy to imagine the speculation, the elaboration, the transformation of such truths and their catalytic effect on audiences eager to shiver with fear at monstrous creatures who haunted far-away lands.

As before, we can take account of the useful observations inherent in this report, and see if they add to our list of vampire characteristics. We can observe first of all, an overall attitude from authorities involved in the investigation which might today be applied to, for example, a road accident or serious local epidemic. The whole matter is taken completely seriously.

1. The situation clearly causes extreme havoc in the local area and is not simply a small event passed by without much concern.
2. In two instances (Arnod Paole and Stana) people are said to have used the blood of the vampire as an antidote to vampirism. In both cases the remedy appears to have failed. From where does this idea arise?
3. People complain that the dead Arnod Paole is terrorizing them at night.
4. The disinterment takes place 40 days after Paole's death. According to medical evidence, the body should not be intact at this point. It is, however, found undecayed, his blood is fresh, and his hair and nails have continued to grow after death.
5. Paole's body is staked and then cremated. Note that the corpse groans and bleeds. The officials, unfortunately, do not witness this directly, but it is noted nevertheless as hear-say.
6. The victims of the vampire are said to become vampires themselves.
7. Vampires attack cattle. Those who eat the cattle also become vampires.
8. Stana's child, who is buried carelessly, is dug up by dogs. This is a revealing piece of information because coffins were introduced due to fears of

vampirism (among other reasons). A body that was accidentally dug up by animals would not achieve departure from this life successfully, thus becoming vulnerable to vampirism.

9. In one of the examples of exhumation, that of Miliza, the body has not remained unchanged but is described as having become plump, whereas before death she was lean. This is an important fact, because, as we shall discover later, quite different, even contradictory conditions, are believed to indicate vampirism.

10. To provide proof that the undecayed bodies are unusual, it is noted, by contrast, that the other bodies have decayed naturally.

11. One vampire (Stanoika) had a mark under the ear. Fluekinger takes this as evidence of throttling, and since it was customary to look for such a mark on the skin of a witch or vampire, this finding would have further confirmed the belief that something unnatural was occurring in the body.

We saw a rather different and quite tragic scene on the same island occasioned by one of those corpses that are believed to return after their burial. The one of whom I shall give an account was a peasant of Mykonos, naturally sullen and quarrelsome, a circumstance to be noted concerning such matters. He had been killed in the fields, no one knew by whom nor how. Two days after he had been buried in a chapel in the town, it was bruited about that he had been seen walking during the night, taking long strides; that he came into houses and turned over furniture, extinguished lamps, embraced people from behind and played a thousand little roguish tricks. At first people only laughed, but the matter became serious when the most respectable people began to complain. Even the Popes acknowledged the fact, and doubtless they had their reasons. People did not fail to have masses said, but the peasant continued his little escapades without mending his ways. After a number of meetings of the town leaders and of the priests and monks, they concluded that it would be necessary in accord with I don't know what ancient ceremony to wait till nine days after the burial.

On the tenth day they said a mass in the chapel where the body lay, in order to drive out the demon that they believed to be concealed in it. The body was disinterred after the mass, and they set about the task of tearing out its

It is easy to see how the legends of the distant past maintain their power
in the human mind, once etched in stone.

heart. The butcher of the town, quite old and maladroit, began by opening the belly rather than the chest. He rummaged about for a long time in the entrails, without finding what he sought, and finally someone informed him that it was necessary to cut into the diaphragm. The heart was torn out to the admiration of all the bystanders. But the body stank so terribly that incense had to be burned. But the smoke, mixed with the exhalations of this carrion, did nothing but increase the stench, and it began to inflame the minds of these poor people. Their imaginations, struck by the spectacle, filled with visions. They took it into their heads to say that a thick smoke was coming from the body, and we did not dare say it was incense. People kept calling out "Vrykolakas" in the chapel and in the square before it, this being the name they give to these supposed revenants. The noise spread through the streets as if it were being roared, and this name seemed to be invented to shake the vault of the chapel. Several of the bystanders claimed that the blood of this unfortunate man was quite red, and the butcher swore that the body was still warm, from which they concluded that the deceased had the severe defect of not being quite dead, or, to state it better, of letting himself be reanimated by the devil, for that is exactly the idea they have of a vrykolakas. They caused this name to resound in an astonishing manner. And then there arrived a crowd of people who professed loudly that they had plainly seen that the corpse had not become stiff, when they carried it from the fields to the church to bury it, and that as a result it was a true vrykolakas. That was the refrain.

I do not doubt that they would have maintained that the body did not stink, if we had not been present, so stunned were these poor people, and so persuaded of the return of the dead. As for us, who had placed ourselves near the cadaver to make our observations closely, we almost perished from the great stench. When they asked us what we thought of the deceased, we answered that we thought him quite adequately dead. But because we wanted to cure their stricken imagination we represented to them that it was not surprising if the butcher had perceived some warmth in the entrails, which were putrefying; that it was not extraordinary if fumes were emitted, just as such emerge from a dung heap when one stirs it up; and as for the pretended red blood, it was still evident on the hands of the butcher that this was nothing but a stinking mess.

After all our reasoning, they were of a mind to go to the seashore and burn the heart of the deceased who, in spite of this execution, became less docile and made more noise than ever. They accused him of beating people at night, of breaking in doors and even roofs, of breaking windows, tearing up clothes and emptying pitchers and bottles. He was a very thirsty dead man: I believe that he did not spare any house but that of the consul, with whom we lodged. However, I have never viewed anything so pitiable as the state of this island. Everyone's head was turned: the wisest people were struck like the others. It was a regular illness of the brain, as dangerous as madness or rage. One saw entire families abandon their houses and come from the outlying areas of the town into the square, carrying their pallets, to pass the night there. Everyone complained of some new insult, and there were nothing but groans at the coming of night. The most intelligent ones withdrew to the country.

In so general a prepossession, we chose not to say anything. They would have treated us not just as fools but as infidels. How is one to bring an entire population back to its sense? Those who believed in their soul that we doubted the truth of the matter, came to us to reproach us for our incredulity and claimed to prove, by authoritative passages from the Shield of Faith of Pere Richard, a Jesuit missionary, that there was such a thing as a vrykolakas. He was a Latin, they said, and therefore you should believe him. Nor should we have got anywhere by denying the conclusion. They made a scene every morning, by the faithful recitation of the new jests committed by this night-bird, who was even accused of having committed the most abominable sins.

Those citizens who were most zealous for the public good believed that the most essential part of the ceremony had been deficient. The mass should not have been said, according to them, until after the heart of this unfortunate man had been torn out. They maintained that, with this precaution, the devil could not have failed to have been surprised, and that without a doubt he would not have returned. Whereas in starting with the mass, they said, he had had all the time necessary to flee and to come back afterwards at his convenience.

After all these reasonings, they found themselves in the same difficulty as the first day. They meet night and day, debate and organize processions for three days and three nights. They oblige the Popes to fast, and one sees them running among the houses, the aspergillum in their hand, sprinkling holy water about and washing the doors with it. With it they even filled the mouth of this poor vrykolakas.

We said so often to the administrators of the town that in a similar situation, in Christendom, one would not fail to establish a watch at night to observe what would happen in the town, that finally they arrested a few vagabonds who certainly had had a hand in these disorders. But apparently they were either not the principal agents, or else they were released too soon, for two days later, to make up for the fast they had undergone in prison, they began again to empty the jugs of wine of those who were so foolish as to leave their houses during the night. Whereupon people were obliged to take recourse again to prayer.

One day, as they recited certain prayers after having planted I don't know how many naked swords in the grave of the corpse which they disinterred three or four times a day, according to the caprice of whomever came by, an Albanian, who happened to find himself in Mykonos, took it upon himself to say, in a professional tone, that it was extremely ridiculous to use the swords of Christians in such a case as this. Can you not see, you poor blind people, he said, that the guard of these swords, forming a cross with the handle, prevents the devil from leaving this corpse! Instead, why don't you rather use Turkish sabers? The opinion of this clever man was of no use: the vrykolakas did not appear to be any more tractable, and everyone was in a strange dismay.

They didn't know which saint to call upon, but with one voice, as though they had given one another the word, they began to cry out, throughout the village, that they had waited too long and it was necessary to burn the vrykolakas entirely. After that they defied the devil to return to set up quarters there. It was better to resort to such an extreme than to have the island deserted. And in fact there were already entire families who were packing up with the intention of retiring to Syra or Tinos. So then they carried the vrykolakas, by the order of the administrators, to the tip of Saint George's Island, where a great funeral pyre had been prepared, with tar, out of fear that the wood, as dry as it was, would not burn fast enough for them on its own. The remains of this unfortunate cadaver were thrown on and consumed in a short time (this was the first of January,

Why is almost every visit to a fictional vampire's castle accompanied by major thunderstorms, lightning and heavy rain?

1701). We saw the fire as we returned from Delos. You could call it a true fire of rejoicing, for one no longer heard the complaints against the vrykolakas. They were content to observe that the devil had certainly been caught this time, and they composed a few songs to ridicule him.

In the whole archipelago people are persuaded that it is only the Greeks of the Orthodox Church whose corpses are reanimated by the devil. The inhabitants of the island of Santorini are terribly afraid of such types of werewolves, and the people of Mykonos, after their visions had dissipated, were equally afraid of prosecution by the Turks and by the bishop of Tinos. Not a single Pope wanted to be present at Saint George when they burned the body, out of fear that the bishop would exact a sum of money for their having exhumed and burned the deceased without his permission. As for the Turks, it is certain that, at their first visit, they did not fail to make the community of Mykonos pay for the blood of this poor devil, who became in every way an abomination and horror to his country.

Beyond the Physical

The most remarkable feature of a vampire is that, though his appearance is human, he has little in common with other men. This strangely enigmatic fact gives the vampire probably his or her greatest power over mere mortals, who naturally possess a passion that is aroused by fugitive beauty, by something that appears real and yet is not; this is the power of a creature which is in effect a human illusion.

Vampires have chosen to live among us exactly because we seem to be obsessed by that which we cannot possess, because we long to attain the impossible, because we fulfil our desires, fears and expectations, and the vacuum in our lives, with what they represent. One could even go so far as to argue that a vampire is a perfectly polished mirror on which we project all our dreams and fancies, sexual and intellectual. This complex projection endows this strange and evil creature with an attraction most of us find impossible to resist.

The movie world has enhanced our mythological past with mysterious horror. Above is Max Scherck as Count Orlok in *Nosferatu* (FW Murnau, 1922).

In order to understand the subtle power that vampires exercise over our psyche, we should look at the tales of men who were ruined by them, whose lives, loves, souls and hearts were stolen by these evil creatures of darkness.

He gazed upon the mirth around him, as if he could not participate therein. Apparently, the laughter of the fair only attracted his attention, that he might by a look quell it, and throw fear into those breasts where thoughtlessness reigned. Those who felt this sensation of awe could not explain whence it arose: some attributed it to the dead grey eye, which, fixing upon the object's face, did not seem to pierce through to the inward workings of the heart; but fell upon the check with a leaden ray that weighed upon the skin it could not pass.

This passage was extracted from Dr. John Polidori's (1795-1821) famous tale *The Vampyre*. Dr. Polidori was the uncle of the future Dante Gabriel and Christina Rossetti and was the youngest man to be awarded a medical degree by the University of Edinburgh. He was also the travel companion to George Gordon, Lord Byron (1788-1824), the great English romantic writer and poet. In 1816 Lord Byron planned a trip across Europe, intending to visit Switzerland, where he would meet with his friends Percy Bysshe Shelley and his wife, Mary Shelley. Polidori was selected to accompany him partly because it was customary to bring along a doctor on such journeys, and partly because of his bright and engaging conversation. But the two men quarrelled often during the trip, and the tension was high when they reached Geneva and were united with the Shelleys.

During a period of nasty weather, the group, to pass the time, began reading some volumes of ghost stories translated from German into French. One day, inspired by the gloom reflected on the stormy waters of Lake Geneva, Byron announced that each would write a ghost story. Mary Shelley dreamed up the idea for her novel *Frankenstein*, which she began at once. Percy Shelley lost interest quickly in the project and wrote nothing. Lord Byron wrote a brief fragment of a story in his notebook. The quarrels between Polidori and Byron continued and eventually the doctor left Geneva. In 1819 a story entitled *The Vampyre* was published in the New Monthly Magazine and was attributed to Lord Byron. The next month's issue, however, contained a letter from Dr. Polidori in which he claimed the story as his own, though he admitted that it was based on the fragments that Byron had begun writing and had abandoned in Geneva. The main character, Lord Ruthven, is apparently based on Lord Byron himself and it offers us many clues as to the intriguing nature of a vampire.

Aubrey, John Polidori's alter-ego in the story, is spell-bound by Lord Ruthven (alias Lord Byron) and decides to observe him closely:

He watched him; and the very impossibility of forming an idea of the charac-
ter of a man entirely absorbed in himself, who gave few other signs of his
observation of external objects, than the tacit assent to their existence, implied

Lord Byron (left) and Mary Shelley (below), two of the midwives of nineteenth century literary vampirism.

Byron's pedigree was a fake, however, for his greatest work of vampirism was in fact written by Polidori.

by the avoidance of their contact: allowing his imagination to picture every thing that flattered its propensity to extravagant ideas, he soon formed this object into the hero of a romance, and determined to observe the offspring of his fancy, rather than the person before him.

This is the first dangerous step into the web that covers the entrance to the vampire's domain: since the creature appears to be 'entirely absorbed in himself,' and since there appears to be no basis for character or personality to anchor any perception of the vampire, then the human mind begins to elaborate, to build upon reality with fantasy, the object (the vampire) becoming the hero of a romance. The second step into the vampire's web is the desire of the human mind to believe in its offspring, or a similar creature to itself, rather than in the reality which it faces; in other words, we prefer to believe in what we create in our fantasies, rather than in what we perceive with our senses. Thus the vampire appears empty, like a shadow, and we, the human observers, may project whatever form will grip our imagination most, truly believing that this is the vampire. In this complex and disturbing fashion the process of depletion begins, and through this balance of fantasy and reality the vampire sucks not only blood, but the psychic energy which controls our mental and physical functions, slowly but surely becoming a perfect projection of our desires.

In folklore, drawn from accounts such as those we have read, the vampire is very different from his fictional counterpart. His colour is never pale, as one would expect from a corpse. His face is commonly described as florid, or of a healthy colour, and this may be attributed to his drinking habits. "The limbs remain flexible, the body is undamaged and swollen up and can give forth fresh blood, the face is red from the blood he drunk ... the eyes are open." We note here that the presence of blood, especially at the lips, may be one of the reasons for the association between vampires and the plague. The pneumonic form of the plague causes the victim to expel blood from the mouth, and the combination of visible blood with unexpected and quite sudden deaths may have led to the belief that vampirism was responsible for the disease.

In some witness accounts we find that the reporters note a peculiarity in the teeth of vampires, "... the lips which are markedly full and red and are drawn back from the teeth which gleam long, sharp as razors, and ivory white." It is also a popular belief in eastern Europe that children born with teeth are destined to become vampires. In this characteristic, the folkloric and the fictional vampires are similar, for they are both believed to use their teeth to extract blood from their victims.

But for all the differences between the appearance in the grave of fictional and folkloric vampires, there is one notable similarity: when found in their graves, both lie quietly in a kind of trance, awaiting their fate. They are not dangerous in this condition, at least until attacked. Their trance points to their non-human nature more than all the physical signs examined so far in this book. There is more to the physiology of a vampire than we have hitherto seen. The creature thus far revealed seems all too physical, but the real vampire possesses characteristics that go beyond the physical nature observed by official witnesses, possessing traits that can only be studied upon embarking on a still more closer examination.

> *Lord Ruthven in his carriage, and amidst the various wild and rich scenes of nature, was always the same: his eyes spoke less than his lip; and though Aubrey was near the object of his curiosity, he obtained no greater gratification from it than the constant excitement of vainly wishing to break that mystery, which to his exalted imagination began to assume the appearance of something supernatural.*

Aubrey observes that Lord Ruthven 'was profuse in his liberality,' though his charitable nature was somewhat questionable since he gave riches to the idle, the vagabond and the beggar, while he turned away the virtuous with sneers of disdain, even though they may have fallen in misfortune. Whenever someone knocked at his door asking for something, 'not to relieve his wants, but to allow him to wallow in his lust, or to sink him still deeper in his iniquity, he was sent away with rich charity.' Lord Ruthven's generosity was, however, of a very sinister nature for 'all those upon whom it was bestowed, inevitably found that there was a curse upon it, for they were all either led to the scaffold, or sunk to the lowest and the most abject misery.'

Lord Ruthven brought the same malice to his relationships with women: all those women who he had sought, apparently for their virtue, had since his departure, 'thrown even the mask aside, and had not scrupled to expose the whole deformity of their vices to the public gaze.'

Lord Ruthven, the vampyre, is a master of psychological manipulation. He plays upon the lust of the wretched by giving them more, so that they end up beyond redemption from vice, and in his intimate relationships with women he has the power to transform even the most virtuous into complete shamelessness. But who could resist his power? The vampire in John Polidori's story appears in classical disguise: a cultured and mannered man of great sophistication and lineage (a lord, no less), a hazy but nevertheless interesting background, and such charisma that few avoid subjugation to it. He spoke of himself as an individual with no sympathy for any other being on the crowded earth, save those to whom he addressed himself, from whom he intended to take, rather than give.

This style of vampire must be the very worst and most cunning of creatures, knowing so well how to use the serpent's art to gain the greatest affection and the deepest trust from those who would be their victims.

In the tale *A Mysterious Stranger* (anonymous, 1860), the vampire describes himself to a party of five horsemen headed by the Knight of Fahnenberg. They had been riding across the Carpathian Mountains to take possession of a castle and lands left in inheritance to the Knight by a childless brother. As evening approached, a fearful northwest wind raged into a powerful storm over the region. Amid the gusts of wind the party could hear the howling of wolves. They were informed by an attendant, who guided them towards their final destination, that at the edge of the wood they were crossing there lay a lake where a pack of fierce wolves dwelt. These wolves had been known to kill even the great bears of the mountains. The howls could be heard more distinctly and closer to the riders than before, and soon they were able to see the eyes of the beasts sparkling in the forest.

The party struggled against the raging storm to reach the end of the wood and sought shelter in the castle of Klatka, which was said to be haunted. Suddenly, just as the Knight and his companions were about to be eaten by the wolves before they could enter the castle gates, a stranger leapt from the shadow of an oak tree and, with a few strides, placed himself between the party and the wolves. As soon as the stranger appeared the wolves gave up their pursuit, tumbled over each other, and set up a fearful howl. The stranger raised his hand, waved it, and the wild animals crawled back into the thickets like a pack of beaten hounds. Without casting a glance at the travellers, who were too much overcome by astonishment to speak, the stranger walked up the castle path and disappeared.

Once the Knight and his companions reached their final destination and had settled in the castle, they began to explore the region on horseback and happened to come to castle Klatka. Here they met the stranger, whom they thanked for having saved them from the wolves. He claimed that the beasts were afraid of him. In order to demonstrate their gratefulness, the Knight invited the stranger to visit them at their new home. The stranger seemed reticent to meet with people and replied, "... besides, I generally remain at home during the day; it is my time for rest. I belong, you must know, to that class of persons who turn day into night, and night into day, and who love everything uncommon and peculiar."

However, a few days later, he presented himself at the Knight's castle in time for supper, when everyone could see him in full view in the brilliantly lit dining chamber,

He was a man of about forty, tall and extremely thin. His features could not be termed uninteresting; there lay in them something bold and daring but the expression was on the whole anything but benevolent. There were contempt and sarcasm in the cold grey eyes, whose glance, however, was at times so piercing that no one could endure it long. His complexion was even more peculiar than his features: it could neither be called pale nor yellow; it was a sort of grey, or, so to speak dirty white, like that of an Indian who has been suffering long from fever; and was rendered still more remarkable by the intense blackness of his beard and short cropped hair. The dress of the unknown was knightly, but old-fashioned and neglected; there were great spots of rust on the collar and breast-plate of his armour; and his dagger and the hilt of his finely worked sword were marked in some places with mildew.

From these descriptions we can get an idea of the non-human qualities of a vampire: a certain detachment from both worldly concerns and human beings; a hardened will which compels him to mock life and all good and virtuous things; the hypnotic stare; the manipulation of feelings and of the psyche; the allurement of victims into an evil world of darkness. These are characteristics that we do not generally meet in everyday life, and whenever a stranger displays them to us we must put our souls on the alert and avoid the alluring vampire's trap which leads to one certainty alone – death.

Chapter 2

Birth of the Undead

ow we take a closer look at how a vampire is born. We know from evidence already set out that these creatures were originally human before undergoing a unique process of transformation – that the vampire body is dead, but remains mysteriously active, functioning for many years, even centuries, unless 'killed' again. We also know that the victims of vampires become vampires themselves – that vampirism is catching, even epidemic, like the plague itself.

But this is not the whole story. There are still unanswered questions. For example, are there prerogatives to vampirism – so to speak 'unnatural' rules laid down by existence which dictate that only certain kinds of victims are chosen to become vampires. Or can any one of us become transformed? And if a vampire feeds on the blood of humans, do all his victims – of which there must be many – become vampires, too, or is there a selection process at work?

The answers to these questions are somewhat confused by the fact that vampires are extremely shrewd and crafty creatures – unwilling to be caught in the act of sinking those razor-sharp canines into the victim's jugular. On the few occasions that first-hand witnesses have been able to swear their presence at a confrontation between vampire and victim, their main concern was to kill the vampire, rather than examining the causes and reasons for the event. In some instances we cannot be sure whether it was the spirit of the dead person which terrorized the community at night and brought death to others, or whether it was the body that came out of the grave, killed at night, and returned to its coffin before dawn. In the eyewitness accounts examined in the previous chapter, we find no remarks on the state of the coffins, whether, for instance, they had been broken open. And since the main witnesses, the victims, are all dead, much of our evidence remains circumstantial.

The best account of the birth of a vampire is given in Anne Rice's exceptional book *Interview with the Vampire*. This extraordinarily detailed account satisfies our thirst for answers and gives a good report of the processes which occur in the body during transformation. This metamorphosis ignores all the natural laws that govern humanity and adopts new ones which permit the body to live outside time and physical deterioration.

In the book, the vampire Louis tells his tale of initiation to a young journalist, in present-day America. He declares that he was made into a vampire at the age of 25 in the year 1791. A terrible tragedy occurred within Louis's family, for which he feels responsible; he is haunted by guilt and loses faith in life and in himself.

> *I drank all the time and was at home as little as possible. I lived like a man who wanted to die but who had no courage to do it himself. I backed out of two duels more from apathy than cowardice and truly wished to be murdered. And then I was attacked. It might have been anyone and my invitation was open to sailors, thieves, maniacs, anyone. But it was a vampire.*

The vampire drains Louis's blood almost to the point of death. The monstrous creature then returns after a few nights, and Louis is so weakened that at first he mistakes him for yet another doctor. But as soon as the vampire's face is visible in the light of the lamp, Louis recognizes that he is no human being.

> *His eyes burned with an incandescence, and the long white hands that hung by his sides were not those of a human being. I think I knew everything in that instant, and all that he told me was only aftermath. What I mean is, the*

Craig Hall in Perthshire, seen from the deep dark forests that lie thickly carpeted below, evoke scenes from Bram Stoker's *Dracula*, in which the terrible Count intended to take up residence in the British Isles. Such a castle as this might have been his choice of residence.

moment I saw him, saw his extraordinary aura and knew him to be no creature I'd ever known, I was reduced to nothing. That ego which could not accept the presence of an extraordinary human being in its midst was crushed. All my conceptions, even my guilt and wish to die, seemed utterly unimportant. I completely forgot myself!... I forgot myself totally. And in the same instant knew totally the meaning of possibility. From then on I experienced only increasing wonder. As he talked to me and told me of what I might become, of what his life had been and stood to be, my past shrank to embers.

Here again we note that the first step into the vampire's domain is through a hypnotic fascination, mainly produced by the promise of eternal life quite outside human values and duties. The longing for oblivion, away from

"His grey eyes burned with an incandescence, and the long white hands that hung by his sides were not those of a human being", as Louis said in the exceptional book *Interview with the Vampire*, by Anne Rice.

mundane preoccupations, pleasures and obligations, must surely be the door through which the vampire is invited into the potential victim's life. To take it, annihilate it, and transform it into something supernatural, into a strange sort of existence that runs parallel to human life and yet is irredeemably separate from it, since its main aim is to feed on it. In a sense, therefore, the wish for eternal life endowed with superhuman power becomes the greatest sin of the ego. And vampirism then, the punishment of such sin.

As Louis, now a vampire, and his initiator Lestat, kill their first victim, Louis becomes aware of why fate chose him for the transformation into a supernatural being,

> *I had seen my becoming a vampire in two lights: the first light was simply enchantment; Lestat had overwhelmed me on my deathbed. But the other light was my wish for self-destruction. My desire to be thoroughly damned. This was the open door through which Lestat had come on both the first and second occasions. Now I was not only destroying myself, but someone else.*

Louis, who still retains some human feelings, wishes to die, for he finds this new form of existence unbearable and abominable. Lestat then attacks him to complete the ritual transformation of a human into a vampire. Louis remembers that the movements of his lips raised the hair all over his body, sending shocks of sensation to every part that was not 'unlike the pleasure of passion'. Louis is blocked to paralysis while Lestat sucks his blood. Then something extraordinary happens to complete the ritual, for Lestat bites his own wrist and gives it to Louis to drink from, for him to savour a vampire's pleasure for the first time.

> *I drank, sucking the blood out of the holes, experiencing for the first time since infancy the special pleasure of sucking nourishment. The body focused with the mind upon one vital source.*

Louis then hears a powerful sound, a roar at first and then something that sounds like the pounding of an enormous drum, as if a great creature was approaching him in a dark and alien forest. And then he hears the pounding of another drum, and the sound of both drums grows louder and louder until it seems to fill his whole body and his senses too. His temples beat at the rhythm of this powerful sound. When Lestat eventually tears his arm free from Louis's bite, the latter realizes that the sound of drums beating was in fact the sound of both their hearts, and that the partaking of each other's blood was a penetration to the very core of one another. After this powerful experience, Louis has passed the threshold from humanity into the supernatural world and starts seeing the world around him through the eyes of mystery.

> *I saw as a vampire… It was as if I had only just been able to see colours and shapes for the first time. I was so enthralled with the buttons on Lestat's black coat that I looked at nothing else for a long time. Then Lestat began to laugh, and I heard his laughter as I had never heard anything before. His heart I still heard like the beating of a drum, and now came this metallic laughter. It was confusing, each sound running into the next sound, like the mingling reverberations of bells, until I had learned to separate the sounds, and then they overlapped, each soft and distinct, increasing but discrete, peals of laughter.*

This is the first account, in fiction, that describes in great detail the way a vampire sees and hears and feels after his transformation. It seems, from what we read, that since the vampire is dead he is also outside the time-frame that governs our own human actions, thoughts and feelings; he is able to feel, hear and sense every event, every detail as if detached from time and time-bound thoughts, and is therefore able to perceive reality in its uniqueness and savour it fully. It appears as though, by having trespassed the curtain of death, the vampire is endowed with a heightened sense of reality. This would make sense, for the vampire is more animal than human; he is a predator, he must kill in order to survive, and therefore he must listen and see everything around him keenly and attentively in order to fulfil his purpose. He has become, furthermore, a supernatural being, and as such he possesses powers that go far beyond the human capacities we rely on for survival.

It is not surprisingly very difficult for us to grasp a thorough understanding of the world of the undead. We are familiar with only three dimensions (height, width and depth), and we have no experience outside this frame. Vampires live in a world of shadows, where matter has neither substance nor importance, where time does not exist, where life is eternal, where powers, unknown and unknowable to us, govern and move in ways that are for us impossible to comprehend. To return to our story, Louis must rid himself of all the human waste in his body, and he goes into the garden to leave behind his last vestiges of humanity:

> When I saw the moon on the flagstones, I became so enamoured with it that I must have spent an hour there... As for my body, it was not yet totally converted, as soon as I became the least accustomed to the sounds and sights, it began to ache. All my human fluids were being forced out of me. I was dying as a human, yet completely alive as a vampire; and with my awakened senses, I had to preside over the death of my body with a certain discomfort and then, finally, fear.

The Revenant

Not all vampire victims become vampires themselves. Vampires need to kill and suck blood, whether from animals or from human beings, in order to survive. The constant fresh blood supply prevents their bodies from wholly decomposing. There is a distinction, however, between a *vampire*, who has undergone a ritual of initiation into vampirism, and a *revenant* (he who returns from the grave), or *undead*, someone who has been attacked by a vampire and had their blood taken, but not to the point of transformation. The revenant dies from shock or eventual loss of blood and is interred, but his spirit appears to his kin and friends or fellow-villagers as a decomposing body, wandering around at night in search of victims. Genuine vampires and revenants share the same method of attack upon their victims: a bite usually to the neck, or in the area of the heart. A revenant transforms all his victims into other revenants, both men and animals, and there is usually a 'vampire epidemic', as slowly but surely the whole village is transformed into a

The revenant dies from shock or eventual loss of blood and is interred, but his spirit
appears to his kin and friends or fellow-villagers as a decomposing body, wandering
around at night in search of victims.

community of revenants. Those who are still alive must then exhume all the bodies suspected to be undead and kill them again to end the epidemic. A vampire, however, has the choice to transform a victim into a vampire through the process of transformation carefully described in Anne Rice's book *Interview with the Vampire*.

> *The victim is never bled to the point of death, is nurtured with great care, is helped to develop the vampire senses until all perception vibrates with high sensitivity, is taught to kill, to search for a coffin, to travel with one across the world without raising suspicion, is taught how to live a wealthy life in the manner of a grand lord or lady. The process of transforming a victim into a vampire can only be described in human terms as a kind of 'falling in love.'*

Thus a vampire leads a very different life from a revenant. The sophistication acquired in the transformation permits him to frequent high social circles and his skills at killing, without being caught, allow him to live for centuries undisturbed. A revenant has a much harder life, since he lacks sophistication and kills anyone and anything, in the open. A revenant is more likely to be caught and killed again than is a vampire.

The revenant's appearance is also quite different from that of the vampire. The vampire has undergone a process of transformation, the putrefaction of the body has been stopped and he or she tends to look intact, however pale and old he may appear. When the vampire is killed his body returns to the natural state of decomposition immediately after the stake enters his heart. A revenant, on the other hand, has no means to prevent his body from decomposing after death, and therefore he looks far more monstrous and repelling.

Trespassing the Gates of Death

> *Lasciate ogni speranza, voi, ch'entrate!*
> (Dante, *Inferno*)
> ("Abandon hope all ye who enter here")

nfortunately, to further our search for empirical evidence, we must now take a closer look at a rather unpleasant feature of vampirism, that of the clinical death of the human body. What exactly do we mean by human death? If we were to treat an ordinary dead body (should we ever have occasion to do so) in the same way as we would treat the body of a vampire, there would be a very different response.

In order to illustrate this rather gruesome statement we must start by examining the physical transformation that takes place after death. I offer an apology for the unavoidably graphic and often unpleasant content of this part of the book, but when we dig deep into the basic nature of vampirism, for all its superficial charm and elegance, it is still associated only with one feature of life: that is, death.

The blood, after death, gravitates into the capillaries of the dependent parts, to impart a pinkish-purple discolouration to the skin, called hypostasis. *If the body is laid supine, the back of the body becomes discoloured. It does not appear in those parts of the body in actual contact with the surface upon which the body rests, for example upon the backs of the shoulders, the buttocks and the backs of the calves. The weight of the body is sufficient to close the capillaries in these areas and prevent them from filling with blood.*

If the body has been lying face downwards, hypostasis affects the front of the body or, in bodies which are suspended, as in hanging, hypostasis first appears in the lower limbs.

Hypostasis becomes apparent about half an hour after death, but it is not complete until some six or eight hours have elapsed. During this time it is possible to change its distribution by altering the position of the body, but, thereafter, the discolouration is usually permanent because the blood has coagulated. Although pink at first, the colour rapidly darkens. When fully developed, hypostasis is dark purple in colour due to the fact that the blood is no longer oxygenated.

When the oxygen in the blood is used up and, as a consequence, the blood becomes darker, one would expect the corpse to become darker as well. But since circulation has ceased, the blood tends to flow, aided by the force of gravity, to the lowest part of the body. The face, then, might be pallid and drained of blood (a popular description of a vampire's countenance) if the body is in a supine position. There are, however, other changes in the colour of the corpse, which are caused by bacterial infection. If, for instance, putrefaction is rapid, as in the case of death brought on by a septic infection, the veins beneath the skin generally become prominent as a bluish-brown network. Changes in colour can also take place with the process medically known as saponification, which preserves the body: the epidermis vanishes during this process, from a combination of decomposition and shedding, and the dermis becomes darkened in bodies interred in coffins, and shades of brown or black appear occasionally.

Recent use of forensic techniques has indicated that one of the most frightening phenomena related to vampirism may have a direct scientific or rather biological explanation.

Recent use of forensic techniques has indicated that one of the most frightening phenomena related to vampirism may have a direct scientific or rather biological explanation. For hundreds of years, grave diggers, exhumers and those working in morgues or hospitals have reported corpses suddenly sitting up some time after death, the body rising elegantly and without hesitation to a sitting position! Not unnaturally such events have caused considerable distress and reports have even been made of witnesses dying from shock or heart attacks as a result.

Until recently these occurrences were put down to supernatural activity, and of course vampirism was a popular cause of the phenomenon, particularly because in a number of cases the bodies actually appeared to slide off the table before collapsing once more.

Within the throat and trachea, there are certain chemicals and fluids that continue to function after death. The body has its own post-death system which continues to work, preparing the corpse for its deterioration and decomposition. Among these fluids there are some that contract at a later point, after the rest of the fluids have dried up, drawing the other organs into this 'dance' of contraction. In effect, the muscles and tissues within the stomach and lower digestive tracts contract and in this process the body arches forwards into a sitting position. If the arms are in a state of rigor mortis at the front of the body, placed across the thighs as is often the case, they will appear to move upwards as they are pushed by the upward movement of the body, thus performing in the classic fashion of the horror movie.

To cut a rather long and disturbing story short, we can sum up the general conditions of the deceased body as follows –

(This listing comes from Glaister and Rentoul's dissertation on the subject and describes the external signs of decomposition.)

- Greenish colouration over the right *ileac fossa* (depression at lowest part of small intestine).
- Extension of greenish colour over the whole abdomen, and other parts of the body.
- Discolouration and swelling of the face.

- Swelling and discolouration of the scrotum, or of the vulva.
- Distension of the abdomen with gases.
- Brownish colouration of the surface veins, giving an arborescent pattern on the skin.
- Development of blisters, of varying sizes, on the surfaces.
- Bursting of blisters, and denudation of large irregular surfaces due to the shedding of the epidermis.
- Escape of blood-stained fluid from the mouth and nostrils.
- Liquefaction of the eyeballs.
- Increasing discolouration of the body generally, and greater and progressive abdominal distension.
- Presence of maggots.
- Shedding of the nails and loosening of the hair.
- Facial features unrecognizable.
- Conversion of tissues into a semi-liquid mass.
- Bursting open of the abdominal and thoracic cavities.
- Progressive dissolution of the body.

Decomposition is aided by the presence of air, moisture, microorganisms, a moderate temperature, and by the presence of insects. The body, however, can be preserved in a number of ways, one of which is burial, intentional or accidental, in lime. When a body is buried in lime, decomposition is retarded and the tissues maintain their suppleness. If we were to put a stick into the hand of such a corpse, it would not be unusual for the dead hand to go on grasping, appearing not to be willing to let go. The reason for this is that the dehydrated hand remains in whatever position

Brownish colouration of the surface veins, giving an arborescent pattern on the skin.

it was placed. And it is evidence such as this that may have frightened exhumers into believing that they were indeed dealing with the body of a vampire, at which point they might well have attempted to kill it again.

When a body that fails to decompose comes to the attention of the populace, then the fact is bound to cause a stir. Historically, we can count two likely explanations given by both Church and populace of this phenomenon: either the body has been reanimated by some extra-human power, a power that acts out of darkness, or the body was the dwelling place of a saint and so was immune to decay. If it was decided that the body was in fact that of a vampire, then it would certainly have to undergo the stake-through-the-heart process.

The Serbian gypsies believed firmly that if a corpse bloated before burial, then it would probably become a vampire.

However, if we refer back to the bodies exhumed by the German officials in the previous chapter, we note an inconsistency. The officials describe the bodies as not being decomposed, but if we use the list given above as a comparison, we can safely state that those bodies were in fact decomposing. In some instances it is noted that the superficial skin had fallen away and that a new, fresher one showed underneath. This could well be the epidermis peeling away and the dermis showing, a clear sign of putrefaction according to Glaister and Rentoul. The underlying dermis is not a new skin, it simply looks raw and possibly redder in colour than the epidermis that covers our bodies in life.

In Greece, for example, the swelling of a body is taken as an unmistakable sign of the presence of a vrykolakas (Greek for vampire). The Serbian gypsies believed firmly that if a corpse bloated before burial, then it would probably become a vampire. Bloating and swelling are viewed as prognostic of the condition of vampirism in the popular mind. Doctors, on the other hand, state that the gases naturally produced within the intestines bloat the body considerably after death. The microorganisms that are formed during decomposition produce gas, mostly methane, throughout the tissues, and since this gas lacks an escape route it collects both in the tissues and cavities. This also explains the 'wild signs,' namely the erections with which the vampires seem to present themselves while lying in the grave.

The emission of blood, or blood-stained fluid, from the mouth and nostrils is also medically explained as the progressive disintegration and putrefaction of the body. The blood coagulates after death but, depending on how death occurred, it either remains coagulated or it liquefies again. This might explain the fact that when the exhumers drove a stake through the heart of the vampire fresh blood issued. Presumably, the common understanding at the time was that blood always coagulated after death, so if it remained liquid then this was another unmistakable sign of vampirism.

This inconsistency gives us, in fact, an important clue in relation to the making of a myth that haunts the dark recesses of our minds, "the vampire has a body, and it is his own body. He is neither dead nor alive; but living in death…" as Montague Summers, a great expert on vampires and in the occult, stated. The outward signs of decomposition in the bodies of vampires are proof of the fact that they are dead; their spirit, however, is still alive, for at night it haunts houses and kills people.

This discovery helps to explain another popular belief on the subject of vampires, namely that when they were alive they were damned, tired of living, and wished for nothing but death. The undead may have been on some occasions victims of misfortune; they may have been murdered, struck by lightning, drowned, or they may have committed suicide. It is these forms of death that brand an individual as one likely to become a vampire, as opposed those who die peacefully in bed. The former unfortunates may also have been left undiscovered for long enough to develop into monsters, growing in size, changing in colour, shedding their skin. If we imagine that these events occurred mostly in rural areas, where communities were held together in

small villages, defending themselves against any evil believed to be lurking in the vast forests that surrounded them, then it is easy to see how something unusual, such as an individual dying on his own outside the village periphery, must have struck a chord of fear and sent the mind spinning into imagined horrors. The very fact that the death was considered primarily as violent and caused by unusual circumstances, was taken as a sign: these people were being punished for their sins on earth. The changes in the dead body would certainly have appeared repulsive and thus confirmed that these beings had lost their human form and had changed into something else... into a vampire. Compulsive fear, or even hysterical terror in the case of vampires, can go in sinister form hand in hand with the causes for misfortune. There are no limits in the fearful mind as to what is considered suspicious behaviour for a corpse!

The gypsies, for instance, state that, "If, after a period of time, the body remains uncorrupt, exactly as it was buried, or if it appears to be swollen and black in colour, having undergone some dreadful change in appearance, suspicions of vampirism are confirmed." Note carefully what is being said in this statement: if the body remains as it was, then it is a vampire, whereas if it changes, then it is also a vampire. The fear of vampires was so great in eastern Europe, that people thought that the best way of recognizing a vampire was to list all possible anomalies in a corpse. Whether it decomposed or not, the only two options a dead body has, it could still be a vampire. The fear was in fact so great that it escapes any logic we might want to find in the criteria used to detect vampirism. There must have been frequent cases in ancient times of mistaken identity when it came to vampire detection.

So we can now conclude, on the basis of the above evidence, that a vampire's body is in fact dead, in the way the vampire Louis explained to the young journalist in Anne Rice's book *Interview with the Vampire*.

We can also see that any deceased body can show the 'unmistakable' signs of vampirism, and especially so those corpses that have remained undiscovered until the process of putrefaction is well under way. As in all legends

Carol Borland and Bela Lugosi in the movie *Mark of the Vampire* (Tod Browning, 1935), evoking the baroque vampire style given birth by John Polidori a hundred years before.

rooted in ancient accounts, our case is hard to prove one way or the other, and the case is still further complicated by the likelihood of mistakes made in the past through lack of precise medical knowledge. We have now seen both sides of the doubter's coin, the mystical and the scientific, so what is the real distinction between an ordinary corpse and a vampire?

The suspicion that a vampire was at work would arise only because of his nightly activities. If other people were dying fast and for unexplained causes, then it was reasonable to assume that someone must be killing them. If no one died and no other distressing events were noticed, then the deceased, however monstrous and repulsive he may have appeared, would presumably not be dug up from his grave.

So to take our investigation a step further and attempt to answer the question of how and in what form a vampire goes on living after death, we must abandon the physical world of death, whose evidence we have at this point exhausted, and enter the veiled world that lies beyond the grave...

Supernature

There have been a number of theories with which scholars have attempted to explain vampires, but these seem as curious as the illogical signs of vampirism we have already examined; moreover, these theories have remained just that – theories. They seem plausible as long as they are not examined too closely, for when we apply the evidence we possess, they tend to fail hopelessly.

According to one prominent theory, vampires are not dead, but merely mortals in a coma and when they come to life after being discovered, they frighten people to such an extent that they are then killed properly. This theory fails because, as we have already seen, the vampires are in a state of decomposition which follows a normal death. In any event, some vampires spent months, if not years, in the grave and it is highly unlikely that they were lying there, sometimes for as long as a century, in a chronic coma. Another, more modern, explanation is offered by Karl Meuli who states that "the quality of our thinking makes it impossible for us to bring about the conception of our non-existence." The villager, terrorized by an epidemic of vampires, was not, however, contemplating his own death, but that of others, and Meuli skirts around this problem by stating that we cannot conceive the death of anyone else either.

We must look elsewhere for our answer, in a domain that is no longer human. Many witness reports indicate that a vampire cannot be actually caught, nor killed while it is walking around, since it is a spirit. The only way of bringing death to the vampire is in the grave, when the spirit has returned to its original abode.

There is a widespread belief that vampires are born with two spirits, one of which is dedicated to the destruction of humankind. In the past, people believed that the spirit resided within the heart, so to kill the evil spirit of the vampire a stake must be driven through its heart, the heart must be cut out and burned, and the ashes must be scattered in flowing water. It was also believed that one could recognize that a vampire has two spirits by the fact that it often talks to itself.

Occultists testify that there exists enough evidence to prove that spirits who are unable to find peace after death come back to reside in a living human body, and in so doing annihilate the individual's spirit and take over

Now I lay me down to sleep,
I pray the Lord my soul to keep;
If I should die before I wake,
I pray the Lord my soul to take.

that body. These evil spirits seek revenge, for they have either died prematurely and are not willing to abandon the earthly life, or they are completing an unresolved task in this world, often an evil one.

There is also the belief within the occult world that the spirit can not only travel and reside in any body of its choice, but that it may take a number of guises. The spirit may, for example, become invisible, or take a white, incorporeal form, or a form similar to the body it inhabits. It can be a breath, a shadow, a light or torch (birthday candles are the modern remnant of this belief). It can be a white dove, or even a bee. If the spirit belongs to an evil person, then it can take the form of a small black dog.

Primitive cultures believe that the spirit is casually attached to its body, for it is reasoned that during sleep, unconsciousness and in death, it leaves the body entirely. The physical changes that the body undergoes during sleep (the slowing down of the pulse and breath) are attributed to the spirit leaving the body. Among the numerous reasons attributed to the dead body's ability to live on is the fact that their image, or spirit, can appear in other people's dreams after they have died.

It is often considered unwise to wake someone up suddenly, for he or she may be dreaming and the spirit may not have the chance to return to the body before it wakes, in which case the person will die. In the eyewitness accounts examined earlier, we saw that many of the victims were visited by the vampire in their sleep; the dreams of choking and blood-sucking were in fact visitations from the undead.

> Now I lay me down to sleep,
> I pray the Lord my soul to keep;
> If I should die before I wake,
> I pray the Lord my soul to take.

This touching prayer has been taught to children worldwide for many centuries; its original meaning (which can be traced back to the twelfth century) was almost certainly connected to the fear of the soul's propensity to be stolen by evil influence.

Mirror Images

Since the soul travels, there are a number of circumstances in which it can remain trapped while out of the body. The popular belief that it is bad luck to break a mirror originates from the idea that mirrors contain the spirit in the form of a reflection. Throughout many parts of Europe, the custom of turning mirrors towards the wall when a member of the household dies is still prevalent. The spirit is thus prevented from reflecting itself and returning to reanimate the body. If a mirror is placed before a vampire there is no reflection, as the spirit is wandering and never present in the body. Our reflection occurs then, not in our physical but in our ethereal presence. In some areas of central and eastern Europe it is considered important to pour out all standing water from containers after a death has occurred, as water can function like a mirror and reflect the soul's image. In Romania all containers of water are covered at night because it is believed that the spirit, while wandering during sleep, might fall into water and drown. The people of Macedonia take the opposite view and leave a container full of water beside a grave to ensure a bad spirit, if it has remained within the grave, is caught should it decide to leave the deceased to torment others at night. In European folk customs we find the practice of pouring water between the corpse and the place where the person died, to provide a barrier between the dead and the living and to prevent the spirit from returning to life. All these customs relate in some way to the original belief that vampires and water don't mix well, and that if a vampire crosses water, the evil spirit will remain trapped in it.

We must remember that most of these customs were developed in pre-industrial Europe, when mirrors were not only scarcely available, but of poor quality. The reflection would have been distorted and ever-changing, and probably no better than in water. Just as mirrors are covered when death occurs and water is used to prevent the spirit from molesting the living, the eyes too are believed to reflect images and thus to capture stray souls. It is, therefore, extremely important to avoid the gaze of a dead man, for death is reflected in his eyes and consequently into the observer's, bringing certain death. And here is the origin of the vampire's hypnotic stare, reflecting death upon the victim and thereby hypnotizing him and enticing him into the vampire's world. Literally staring the victim to death. In funerary rites we can still observe the practice of closing the eyes of the deceased. Our modern interpretation of this ritual is to give sleep to the dead, but the original purpose was to avoid the reflection of death upon the living.

Many cultures believe that 'the other world' is quite literally a mirror image of this world. Everything is upside-down by comparison with this world. The spirit world is reached by movements contrary to the normal: in fact, devil worshippers read the Lord's Prayer backwards as part of their Black Mass.

What is good here, is evil there. Matter corresponds to shadow, life to death, high to low, and so on. Souls of the other world seek to come back and take possession of a dead body in order to go on living.

Often, the spirit leaves the body at the point of death but decides to come back, reanimating the body to create a vampire. For this primitive and long established reason, the living will take steps to ensure that the spirit is successful in leaving the body: doors and windows are opened, the house is swept clean, the dust and dirt put outside to safeguard against the possibility that the soul is hidden in a corner somewhere.

Hidden Practices

If we examine funereal practices carefully, we can see that the rites of transition and of incorporation of the deceased into the world of the dead are not only elaborate and complex but very often hide meanings that we have either long forgotten or found alternative, more rational reasons for. They have been developed over the centuries to ensure that the spirit completes its journey safely to the other side, that it rests in peace there forever, and that it does not come back to take other lives with it.

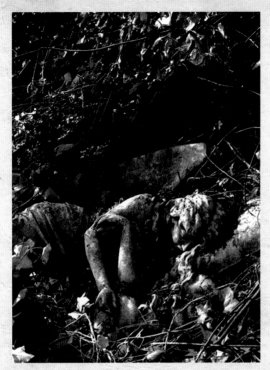

A fallen angel beside an old grave. Hungry vampires used
the graveyard as a last resort to find fresh bodies recently
buried, their blood still uncongealed, in the days when the
dead were thrown unceremoniously into the ground.

We might, for example, consider the function of mourning in a different
light. It is normally seen as an expression of sorrow and respect for the
deceased, but many cultures view it as a necessity, not a courtesy. The length
of the mourning corresponds to the period in which the corpse is thought
to be in a dangerous position, for fear of the return of the spirit. In southern

Italy and Spain, women mourn ten years for their fathers and husbands and five years for their brothers and sons. Often, professional mourners are hired. Many women even change their appearance; they no longer wear makeup, they cut their hair and wear black clothes for the entire mourning period. The mourning clothing and change of hairstyle were originally intended to

The gravestone was placed above the head of the body in the grave so that, if a returning spirit should occupy the dead, the body would not be able to sit up. Only criminals, alcoholics and great sinners were not accorded formal burial, just the sorts of characters one might expect to be occupied by floating souls! Where there was no gravestone, a vampire could come to life again. Where there was moral weakness, life could last forever.

render unrecognizable those who were left behind. If the dead person was to return, he or she would fail to recognize their first potential victim, the husband or wife they left behind.

These widespread beliefs and practices testify to the idea that the spirit is in fact quite separate from the body. A vampire can have one of two spirits; one which is evil and may take over from the naturally resident spirit in a living body; or one that has risen from a body and returns there to the putrefying corpse, taking possession of it by reanimating it, and carrying on living as long as it can find enough victims to feed on.

Legend provides us with some glorious circumstances under which vampirism may occur, both the vampire's reasons for being born and the environments, causes and circumstances of their birth.

Disposed to be a Vampire

Those who are different from others, those who are unpopular, or great sinners, form the most likely candidates either to be taken by vampires or to come back from the dead. In eastern Europe, for instance, alcoholics are believed to be prime candidates for vampirism, and in Russia people were exhumed after burial just because they were alcoholics when alive.

Those who commit suicide are firmly believed to come back from the dead and claim new lives. In the past, they were refused burial in a church-yard and even these days suicide is still considered a crime.

Christians who convert to Islam are believed, in some countries, to become vampires, as are priests who say Mass in a state of mortal sin, as well as children whose godfathers stumbled upon reciting the Apostles' Creed at their baptism.

In general, witches, sorcerers, the godless, the evil-doers, werewolves, robbers, arsonists, prostitutes, deceitful and treacherous barmaids, and other different and dishonourable people have the potential to come back from the dead and take the guise of a vampire. It is interesting to note that this is reminiscent of the idea of good and bad karma which is prevalent in Eastern cultures. In the East, particularly in India, the life of an individual, if it is considered badly managed through crime or misdeeds, may dictate the quality of the next life. An alcoholic may be forced to deal with his indulgence in his next life, likewise a criminal. The tradition that believes in the chance of a soul returning to a second life, this time of vampirism and thus punishment of the worst kind, has a similar basis.

Destined to be a Vampire

Very often people become vampires through no fault of their own. Among them are those that were conceived during a holy period according to the Church calendar, and the illegitimate offspring of illegitimate parents. Potential vampires can also be recognized at birth, usually by some abnormality. Examples include when a child is born with teeth, with an extra nipple, with a lack of cartilage in the nose (remember the fallen nose in one of the vampire accounts), with a split lower lip, or with features that are viewed as bestial, such as fur down the front or back, or a tail-like extension of the spine, especially if it is covered with hair. If a child is born with a red caul, or amniotic fluid, then it is regarded in many parts of Europe as predestined to become a vampire. The caul is, under normal circumstances, white. If it is red it must be dried up, stored and crumbled into the child's food after a fixed period of time in order to prevent vampirism.

Made to be a Vampire

The vampire does not always suck blood from the victim's neck; it may attack the thorax, the left breast, the area of the heart, or the left nipple. In China and throughout the Slavic countries it is believed that a dead body may become a vampire if an animal such as a dog or cat, or anything animate, including even a man or woman, jumps over it. If a bat, in particular, flies over a body then there is no escape from vampirism. Likewise if an individual's shadow is stolen, then he will become a vampire for sure. The theft, according to the most common legend, tends to occur in or close to buildings, where the shadow is seen clearly against a wall and then caught by driving a nail through its head.

If the deceased cannot be buried, either because Mother Earth will not accept the burial, like with evil-doers who are believed to be unwanted by the earth, or because the authorities would object, then it is more than likely that the poor victim will return as a vampire.

Vampire's Undoing

There are, of course, many human failures that will lead to the birth of a vampire. Not surprisingly, one example is carelessness in the carrying out of funeral rites. For example, it is considered dangerous for a corpse to be left unattended. Likewise, if the body is buried without a priest, then it is likely to come back. Lack of burial altogether, however, is the surest sign that the deceased will become a vampire.

Chapter 3

The Ways of the Vampire

Progress Towards Immortality

The vampire has traditionally led a somewhat withdrawn, perhaps even quiet, uncomplicated life. Once he has completed the process of transformation and perhaps lived some years in relative poverty while building up his skills and connections, his next task is to acquire a castle in some remote area, or a grand residence suitable to keep both his coffins and his victims in a location unlikely to attract attention. He is also concerned with preventing the local populace from suspecting the nature of his ways and, at least in the past, a lord was more privy than a commoner, especially in the remote districts of eastern Europe.

He usually enjoys a parasitic relationship with those who live in the local area, as it is occasionally necessary for him to draw upon human flesh in the district for his continued pleasure and survival. This is a potentially dangerous situation for him, for although he does not wish to be thought greedy and therefore a danger to the maintenance of local population figures, he does want to maintain a certain aura of mystery and doubt among his neighbours as a deliberate policy to keep them in a subdued state of fear for their safety. This gives him freedom to feed off the occasional virgin, young man, or other juicy morsel. In many eastern European districts, the very name of his castle, when uttered by a visitor, may send the neighbours into a state of distress. Organised action on the part of the local population is unlikely, however, due to a general apathy, some will say brought about by the hypnotic cloud cast by the Lord vampire himself.

Intrinsic Perils

The lifestyle of the vampire could perhaps be described as aesthetic. In order to maintain his aura of mystery, as we have seen, he lives on the borders of society, maintaining a low profile and so has very little contact with others of his kind, except those that he keeps entrapped for his pleasure.

He is often an intellectual. His extremely long life, after all, permits him a considerable knowledge of the world around him, of culture, literature, art and even music, though doubtless his tastes in these things will be suitably dark in character, perhaps leading him to adorn his castle walls with Giotto rather than Michelangelo.

He functions in the local ecosystem for hundreds, or even thousands, of years carefully maintaining the fine balance between his need for fresh blood and the local supply. He is often a great expert in local heritage and the history of local feuds and mysterious deaths, since he has likely perpetrated a good many of the deaths himself. He will astound visitors with the extent of his detailed knowledge of events, for indeed he enjoys the mimicry of the human ego greatly and probably excels at the majority of human gifts.

There are a few problems, however, that the vampire must address if he wants to live like a man, rather than wander in woods and deserted places. First of all he does not eat at all, nor does he exist in public during the day.

The dark forces of the devil took many forms but they were all born out of the fear of death and damnation. Vampirism and witchcraft almost always went hand in hand in medieval Europe.

Servants who have suspected their masters of vampiric practices, have revealed sightings through key-holes of charade-like dinners with empty plates, the lifting of an empty glass to dry lips and the pretence of cutting food by the scratching of the plate with unblemished silver.

The vampire must also pretend to suffer a great number of sicknesses and indispositions which prevent him from seeing people during the day. Why pretend, one may ask, if one is endowed with richness and eternal life? But the vampire is often made scapegoat for otherwise inexplicable phenomena.

Not only are mysterious deaths attributed to him, but also floods, famines, harvest failures and any variation of normal life, otherwise unexplained. The following verse, drawn from Galician folklore, testifies to the all-embracing power of the vampire:

> The power of the vampire is very great and many-sided, even in his lifetime he can kill people and even eat them alive; can bring into being, or remove, various sicknesses and epidemics, storms, rain, hail and such; he casts spells on the cows and their milk, the crops and the husbandry generally; he knows all secrets and the future etc. Besides this he can make himself invisible or transform himself into various objects, especially into animal forms.

These lines illustrate the flexibility of ancient legend. The writer attempts to document the powers and doings of the vampire, ending the sentences with 'etc' and 'and such,' thus providing sufficient poetic license to those who follow to extend them as needed.

A Vampire's Convenience

The seclusion of his daytime rest is, of course, of the utmost importance. The coffin requires a hiding place of absolute security, for generally he is most vulnerable while within it. This aspect of the vampire's life reminds us that he is most at home in death and yet still, as are all the dead, most prone to danger. The coffin itself will perhaps be lined with fine silk, but must always have a layer of soil from the native grave in which the vampire was interred at his death. The trappings of his death process are always required and the original earth is a part of this: the earth to which he should have gone dust to dust, ashes to ashes, almost as though he inevitably accepts that final destruction must come.

The servant most readily available to a vampire is likely to be a revenant. The vampire maintains his servant in a perfect balance between life and death, maintaining trust through service and in return being helped against ultimate decay, for without the vampire's continued attention the revenant would certainly deteriorate as we have described before. The servant pledges his will to serve his lord and acts as if he were perpetually hypnotized, keeping curious visitors, such as students of the occult or inquiring doctors, at bay and providing a constant supply of rats and other small animals for fresh blood, barring all doors and access to the master's place of rest, and making sure that when he is away from home, the conditions necessary to the life of his master are maintained. This servant is probably the only one with a close relationship with the vampire, for he is permitted to witness the whole truth of his master's life.

Otherwise the vampire is a lonely creature who must live in isolation, kill and drink blood, commit horrendous acts of inhuman behaviour, and yet still possess human feelings. He will never, over centuries, come in contact with other creatures with whom he might share thoughts, feelings, sensations. Two vampires could never live together, for their need to kill would soon exhaust the local supply of fresh blood, and their unparalleled lust for the fluid of human life would bring them constantly in conflict with one another.

The Bloodlust of the Countess Bathory

Perhaps one of the most famous cases of the vampire's lust for blood and power was that of the Countess Erzsebet Bathory of Hungary, whose life has been portrayed in many stories and even on film. She is said to have drunk and bathed in the blood of 650 young virgins in the belief that the practice would rejuvenate her. Victims were recruited, with the help of her subordinates,

Countess Erzsebet Bathory of Hungary, the beauty and the beast.

on the pretense of recruiting servant girls at the Castle Csejthe, her home. All of them, inevitably, fell prey to her insatiable lust for blood. In the winter of 1610, however, the castle was raided after an intended victim had escaped and warned the authorities of the crimes committed by the Countess. Blood-drained bodies were discovered, some pierced with tiny holes all over the flesh; some girls were found alive, but partially drained, and one was found completely emptied of blood, but still warm. Her accomplices were tried and beheaded, and the Countess was walled up in her own bedroom and fed through a small hole until she died in 1640. It is still not known whether the Countess was a true vampire or simply an insane woman with a particular passion for youth. There are those who live near the spot on which her castle stands in ruins who say she still walks and still kills.

Today it is becoming increasingly difficult for a vampire to find a remote area with a castle where he can live peacefully and enjoy a local community of villagers to supply him with the fresh blood he needs for sustenance.

Driven by hunger, vampires have been known to sweep cities and their suburbs in search of victims. In 1980 the *Weekly World News*, an American newspaper, revealed in its December 2nd issue under the heading "Vampire Killings Sweep the U.S." the following:

A terrifying wave of vampire killings is sweeping the nation, and experts believe that the bloodthirsty murderers may be responsible for as many as 6,000 deaths a year.

Police are investigating dozens of eerie murders which have left pale, broken bodies of victims drained of blood, sometimes horribly mutilated and bearing the evidence of ghoulish Satanic rituals.

They include:

— A double murder in New York City in which the victims were so completely drained of blood that the medical examiner could not get enough for a blood sample.

— Six Sacramento, California, people who were murdered by a man who later admitted drinking the blood of his victims.

— A seven-year-old Bronx, New York, boy who was found hanging upside

An image of the vampire today taken from *Lat den ratte komma in* (*Let the Right One In*), a Tomas Alfredson film based on the 2004 novel by Swedish horror writer John Ajvide Lindqvist.

down, the blood drained from his horribly mutilated body.

– Nine hobos who were killed in California, each on the night of the full moon, by a murderer who also drank their blood.

"There is no doubt that these creatures need as much human blood as a pint a day," said Dr. Stephen Kaplan, Chief of the Vampire Research Center in Elmhurst, New York "They can't buy it. It requires a prescription. I believe that these people sometimes grab hitch hikers to satisfy their blood lust."

We cannot be sure, of course, that this is the work of vampires or revenants at all, but simply some crazed human beings. Nevertheless, there are sufficient reports of this nature across the world each year for us to believe that at least some of them are the work of authentic vampirism. The legend is kept very much alive even today.

Dressing for Dinner

vampire can live for hundreds, or even thousands, of years. During this time he is able to collect considerable wealth and a proper status amid the more obscure titles of noble families. As he undertakes to live the life of a lord, he must dress accordingly. To get round the problem of being indisposed during the daytime, and therefore unable to visit local hatters and tailors, the vampire will, instead, richly reward those who open the doors of their stores after dark, as well as those who are prepared to meet in elegant restaurants in the small hours of the night to conduct economic transactions. The illustrations on these pages may well represent the modern equivalent of the best-dressed vampire, one that we might not even recognize as a vampire, except on closer examination.

The traditional vampire dresses as a gentleman. The most common attire, familiar to all, is the long black cape that, when opened, resembles the shape of the wings of a vampire bat. (Incidentally, vampire bats were named after

"I condemn you to living death. To eternal hunger for living blood!"
Dressing for dinner, Gary Oldman in *Bram Stoker's Dracula*, the Francis
Ford Coppola film (1992).

vampires, not vice versa. The story that a vampire will become a bat at night
is untrue.) The fabric of the cape is a satiny, shiny, slippery silk, and no investigation has yet been able to identify exactly its quality and origin. Some say
it is woven by the vampire himself after final discovery of his transformation,
the secret being handed down from vampire to vampire, never to be revealed
to mortal humans. The vampire can envelope his entire body and head within
the folds of his cape, slightly raising his arms above the head in a pose which
has become familiar to most of us. In so doing he creates, for the human
onlooker, a 'black hole', making himself literally invisible. In this guise he can
hide anywhere, or leave altogether unseen.

Beneath the cape the vampire wears an elegant black tuxedo, with long
tails which reach to below his knees. His sharply pressed trousers are, of
course, also black.

The tuxedo is invariably worn with an evening shirt and a stiff collar,
spotlessly white, the collar noticeably higher than normal in order to disguise
the deathly pallor of his face. The vampire will never show himself in full
light, but chooses only candlelit rooms, the fashion of his garments camou-
flaging his true appearance.

The tuxedo, trousers and evening shirt are also fashioned from the same
sleek material as the cape in order to facilitate swift movement. He is also
aided by the fact that he lives outside human time, and his bodily movements
are therefore extremely rapid. So fast, in fact, that they become almost imper-
ceptible to the human eye.

To accompany the elegant garments, he will wear patent leather shoes,
polished to perfection by his hypnotized attendant.

As a modern break with tradition, we have, on these pages, added some
more extravagant fashion to the vampire's wardrobe. The modern
vampire, after all, with so many centuries of learning, permits himself the
indulgence as well as the camouflage of modern-day disguise.

Chapter 4

In Search of
Count Dracula

The most famous fictional portrait of the aristocratic vampire is found in the novel *Dracula* by Bram Stoker. Stoker was the first to bestow this musical-sounding name to the monster and Dracula was, thereafter, to be immortalized in numerous feature films and fictional stories as the archetypal vampire: aristocratic, disturbingly ugly, always pale and gaunt, an emaciated creature with pointed ears and long fingernails, dressed in a black cape and tuxedo, one who entices his victims by hypnotizing them with his stare and whispering softly in that thick Hungarian accent.

Dracula was for a long time thought to be a product of the wild imagination of Bram Stoker. However, the outstanding and extremely detailed geographical, historical, topographic and folkloric context in which the novel is set leads us to believe that Stoker may have undertaken the journey from London to 'Dracula country' himself, or may have done extensive research on eastern Europe and Romania before writing the work.

Count Dracula is based on the character and deeds of a legendary Romanian prince, known to historians as Vlad Dracul the Impaler, whose fame as a ruthless, clever and bloodthirsty prince and leader of armies crossed the borders of Romania and reached central Europe and even England,

The legendary Romanian prince, known to historians as Vlad Dracul the Impaler, whose fame travelled across Europe.

Stoker's native soil. Vlad Dracul lived in a rural region of Romania called Transylvania, and ever since the publication and success of Stoker's novel the area has been identified as Dracula country. Many a vampire hunter, as well as students of the occult, medical doctors, and simply curious tourists have undertaken the journey to research and discover a glimpse of the famous Count, to study his ways and habits, or even to put an end to his murderous existence. With the passing of time, Vlad Dracul has come to be identified with his fictional reflection, Dracula the Vampire.

A Journey into Dracula Country

To embark upon the vampire trail is to undertake a journey of mystery and danger which leads us to a country that looks and feels like those lands we dream of in fairy tales: great expanses of dark and thick forest across the Carpathian mountains, and into the misty and remote valleys of Transylvania, on the hills of which stands Dracula's castle, eerie with the memories written on its walls of past impalements, torture and cruel and bloody deeds.

We provide here a guide for the traveller, warning him or her that this should on no account be treated as a holiday, for it will open doors to matters that mankind has never seen or lived through before.

From New York or London, or indeed any other city in the world, the first stop must be Munich, that beautiful city in Bavaria, Germany. On arrival in Munich, seek out the Hotel of the Four Seasons (Vierjahrzeiten Hotel):

This fabulous map of Transylvania was prepared by one of the most important cartographers of its time, Coronelli. The map is based on the one printed in 1688 and shows the cities and villages with their Hungarian, German and Romanian names.

Jonathan Harker, the main character in Bram Stoker's novel, stayed there, as did all the other explorers and vampire hunters in history. The hotel is one of the main stepping stones in the vampire trail: its glorious rooms invite one to collect one's thoughts and to prepare for the adventure into the wilderness.

From Munich we climb aboard the express train to Austria's capital city Vienna. The journey takes us through some of Europe's most startling and beautiful country, and from Vienna we continue on to Budapest, in Hungary. Vienna and Budapest sit on opposite banks of the Danube and the train journey follows the large and slow curves of this great flowing river.

The magnificent city of Budapest is the gateway to eastern Europe, a newly opened world following the recent fall of communist suppression. It is also the last post of central Europe, and from here on the traveller enters the real eastern borders of the continent, quickly becoming enveloped in an atmosphere of romance and mystery, for this part of Europe is truly and recognizably different from any other, drawing the traveller back into a time when vampires really did have sway over the villages and people. Primitive, basic times filled with high winds and strong fears which still live in these often bleak lands. From Budapest the journey continues to Cluj in Romania, approximately six hours by train to this the largest city of Transylvania. In Stoker's novel, Cluj is named 'Klausenburgh', the Anglicized German spelling of the name, since in his time this area was within the jurisdiction of the Habsburg Empire. Jonathan Harker, the hero of Stoker's novel, stayed at the Hotel Royal, today called the Continental.

Cluj represents the heart of Transylvania, a city of extremely ancient ethnic mixes of population: the Saxons in the south, the Wallachians (or Romanians), the Magyars (or Hungarians) in the west, and the Szekelys in the east and north, who claim to be descended from Attila and the Huns. The name Romania originates in the ethnic origin of its population, for this area was the eastern most province of the Roman Empire. The native language of the Roman soldiers stationed there was Latin, and the Romanians take pride in their Latin roots, a unique heritage in eastern Europe, where the spoken tongues are largely Slavonic.

The Romanians are strangely cautious, shy people who have very largely retained their gentle peasant ways, particularly in the countryside. The recently ended dictatorship under the dreaded Ceausescu family has left its mark on the land and the people, holding them almost as though in a frozen state of development. Ceausescu himself was thought to have been a vampire, perhaps, according to the still-told stories of outlying areas, still walking at night in search of victims. In any event the atmosphere of Romania satisfies the vampire-hunter's desire of uncertainty and adventure, the glorious scenic value of the land somehow undercut with shadow.

After a good night's rest, the traveller will take heart in tasting the local *mamaliga*, a sort of porridge of maize flour, which remains the national and very nutritious dish of the Romanian peasant. For his lunch in Cluj, Jonathan

Here comes that dark, shadowy figure once again, lurking in the places we would be ill-advised to venture. In this case, the most popular Dracula, Bela Lugosi.

Harker partook of paprika chicken and *umplutura*, an aubergine dish. These dishes are so much part of the culinary fare of Transylvania that it is said that even Count Dracula offers them to his guests, while he remains seated in the inimitable stillness of the meditating vampire without tasting anything, of course, for his diet is somewhat restricted.

From Cluj it is possible to enter Dracula country only by car. The journey to Bistrita takes about a day. The surrounding area is largely forests of oak, beech and pine. Gentle streams break the greenness of the valleys and altogether the view is so pleasing to the eye that it is hard to imagine how movie makers depicted it as a sinister, bleak, primeval and dangerous landscape. Every now and then, one can see a castle or a hill-fort perched on top of a steep hill. Haystacks are neatly piled by farm workers on the edges of the cultivated fields, and the farms can be identified by chimney smoke late in the afternoons, when the work is finished and the men and women return home for a cup of warm soup after their hard day.

The people of Transylvania are both deeply religious and superstitious: by the side of the road the traveller will notice many crosses to protect the road and the fields at the side, but also to bless and protect workers and travellers.

Students of folklore will assert that superstitions abound in this northern part of the country, where the local villagers still believe that the forces of good and evil are constantly fighting for supremacy, taking in their stride human destiny and action. There is little science here to break the pattern of mystery. The peasants believe, for instance, in *nosferatu*, or *necuratul*, which literally means 'the unclean one' and in Romanian applies to the devil. The *Ordog* in Hungarian, meaning Satan, is believed to roam around the dark forests at night. It would be inadvisable to utter the word *strigoiaca* (meaning female vampire) in Romanian for it is believed that, being more mischievous than her male counterpart, she will appear as soon as she is summoned and take a life with her. The word 'vampire' derives from the Slavic *vampyr*, a creature well known to the Romanian peasant. The villagers have recourse to the powers of the church (holy water, the cross and prayers), as well as herbs such as garlic, wolfbane and petals of wild roses which are grown to combat their fears and to send away the evil creatures when they appear. There is nothing in this that the Romanian farmer would laugh at, for the conditioning of history is too long and unbroken to be termed superstition. It is only Westerners who describe it so, degrading its value. One visit to this extraordinary country is enough to convince anyone that there are more things in heaven and earth than we could possibly be aware of in our restricted Western philosophy. For this is the land of the vampire, first and before all else.

Bistrita is located in the extreme east of the country near the border with Moldavia and Ukraine, deep in the Carpathian mountains. From Bistrita we can proceed across the pass of Prundul-Bargaului. The description of the area in Bram Stoker's novel is still accurate today.

Before us lay a green sloping land full of forests and woods, with here and there steep hills, crowned with clumps of trees or with farmhouses, the blank gable end to the road. There was everywhere a bewildering mass of fruit blossom – apple, plum, pear, cherry; and as we drove by I could see the green grass under the trees spangled with the fallen petals.

Home of the Blood Drinker

It is at Borgo Pass (the Anglicized name for Prundul-Bargaului) that the traveller finally reaches Dracula's castle.

… a vast ruined castle. From whose tall black windows came no ray of light, and whose broken battlements showed a jagged line against the moonlit sky.

It is here that the Count, 'a tall, old man, clean shaven save for a long white moustache' lives. He is clad in black from head to foot, possibly in the fashion of a local nobleman of the time. He states,

Here I am noble; I am boyar; the common people know me, and I am master.
(The word boyar, a Slavic word, refers to a member of the land-owning nobility in the Romanian language.)

Count Dracula created a 'forest of the impaled' which lined the roads to welcome invading troops, and indeed all visitors, at the borders of his country.

Once again we find representation of death etched forever – as though the sculptor wished to remind us of our deepest fears.

We do not know, truly, whether Dracula still lives in Romania. The fictional character in Stoker's book was clearly based on the real-life Vlad Dracul, a man of immense capability, power and violence, who is documented to have remained alive for more than two hundred years. In Bram Stoker's story Van Helsing, the vampire-hunter who courageously follows Jonathan Harker's footsteps from London to Bistrita to find and kill Dracula, gains knowledge of the vampire from his friend Arminius of Buda-Pesth. Arminius Vambery was also a real man, a notable scholar and orientalist, and a contemporary of Bram Stoker, who often travelled from Budapest to London and deposited his studies on vampirism at the British Museum, at that time the largest library and source of knowledge in the world. Arminius Vambery seems to have discovered a rare document in which Count Dracula was referred to as a 'wampyr, which we all understand too well.' The word in essence means 'blood-drinker.'

In the novel, Count Dracula's ancestry goes back to 'wolf country.' The Dacians, Romanian ancestors, often described themselves as 'wolf-men' and their banner was the head of a wolf with the body of a snake.

Count Dracula is described by Van Helsing as possessing a 'mighty brain, and to be an erudite of new tongues, politics, law, finance, science and even of the occult,' all attributes that the Count shares with his historical alter-ego, Vlad Dracul. Was Vlad Dracul the first well-known vampire in history, on whose character, lifestyle and deeds the legends were moulded and grown? Or is Count Dracula the still-living Vlad Dracul, surviving as a vampire for hundreds of years, and silently domiciled in Romania?

Dracula the Impaler

Dracula gained fame far beyond his position in world politics, greater even than his time in history, a rough and dangerous period beset by constant war, almost as dreadful as our own. He was infamous in Romania and its neighbouring countries during his lifetime for committing the worst crimes history had ever known; worse, some say, than the crimes committed by Caligula in Rome. He created a 'forest of the impaled' which lined the roads to welcome invading troops and indeed all visitors at the borders of his country. Pregnant women, children, young and old men were staked, the sharp poles thrust between their buttocks, the body being pulled downwards until the sharp point appeared through the throat or top of the head, the wooden pole was then planted in the monstrous forest. This was the first sign to deter anyone, intended to prevent crime or treason against the terrible Dracul, leader of this wretched country. When emissaries refused, out of custom, to remove their hats in his presence, he told them that he wished only to honour and strengthen their custom, and nailed the hats to their heads, a cruelty that Ivan the Terrible of Russia was later to adopt.

After Dracul's apparent death, his cruel reputation was spread across the lands on the tongues of monks travelling from Romania to the German and Austrian provinces. Military leaders emulated some of his war techniques, also hoping to emulate his success in fighting back the Turkish armies who, throughout his reign, constantly threatened invasion of his country.

His bloodthirsty nature became the subject of the first horror stories ever to be published in fifteenth-century central Europe, and the reading offered such wicked pleasure to the public that these early books became international

Whether a heroic leader of armies or a cruel monster, Dracula seems to be still more interesting than his fictional romantic counterpart.

bestsellers at the time, selling nearly as many copies as the Bible. Whether he was a heroic leader of armies or a cruel and ruthless monster, Vlad Dracul the Impaler seems to have been even more interesting than his fictional romantic counterpart. Following extensive research carried out by vampire hunters and other scholars interested in the subject, this man can now be revealed in a clear light and judged fairly within the historical context of the ravaged times in which he lived.

The Dracula Clan

Prince Dracula, who ruled the territories that in modern times fall within Romania, was born in 1431. Europe, which extended at the time from the Atlantic Ocean to the Black Sea and the Baltic coast, represented much more than a united civilization. Powerful dynastic ties of vassalage and honour linked countries together and, even though the Renaissance had made its mark upon European culture, the Church still had an all-pervasive authority and the strata of society were still locked in the tight grip of the feudal structure. Dracula's birthplace, Transylvania, is a region that was inhabited from ancient times by the Daco-Romans or, as they came to be called in more modern times, Romanians. Having been conquered by Rome in AD 101 and AD 105, the Dacians, the original inhabitants, gave up the struggle and the area was incorporated into the Roman Empire and witnessed massive immigration with people coming from all corners of the Empire. The region is located beyond the Carpathian mountains and was described by early chroniclers who travelled there as 'trans-silva' which in Latin means literally 'across-forest'. The Carpathian mountains are densely forested and the name gives an exact visual description of the region.

Because of its geographical position, in very close proximity to the Black Sea and the territories of the Ottoman Turks to the southeast and of the Tatar's Golden Horde to the northeast, Transylvania and the whole region, known today as Romania, was very vulnerable to invasion by the infidels who, by conquering these territories, would have free access to all of central Europe. Romania was in a similar position to some regions of the Middle East today, a flashpoint of political turmoil.

Turkish invasions led to widespread destruction, burning of villages and fields, and the killing of large numbers of the population. But the Turks not only brought death in the form of war, they also brought terrible diseases such as syphilis, tuberculosis, leprosy and smallpox. These ravagings, together with natural calamities such as floods, bad harvests, earthquakes and swarms of locusts imported from the East, moved the inhabitants of these remote regions into a state desperation and a great reliance on what we now call superstition. They believed firmly in the power of evil, which could only be combated by the consultation of oracles and soothsayers. Travellers to eastern Europe at the time reported a great belief in 'false' idols, the burning of witches and all other kinds of superstitious behaviour.

This then is the climate that formed the cultural cradle to the young Vlad Dracul, the true-life model for the Prince of Darkness. But be careful not to judge (in the same way as perhaps Victorian or even more modern travellers have done) that historical background, for as we have seen a great many of the traditions and legends of these people were grounded in a very practical requirement: the presence of mystery as a force towards understanding. Evil was as real a presence in their lives as the land around them, the harvest and the clothes they wore. It arrived on their doorsteps in the form of constant war, poverty and struggle, and the witches' or shamanic magic they believed in was a very real form of understanding, working in not dissimilar ways to our modern scientific values. This all, to them, was very real. Among Vlad's ancestors was Mircea the Great, his great-grandfather, who became famous in history for his diplomatic skills and for successfully conquering new territories. His main seat of power was Wallachia, a region bordering Transylvania. In order to avoid submission to the Turks, Mircea the Great signed a treaty of alliance with Sigismund of Luxembourg in 1395. After the treaty, Mircea took part in a crusade led by Sigismund against the Ottomans.

It was customary at the time to send sons of noble families to be trained and instructed by other nobility for a number of years and, usually, the two families had vested interests or were linked by a tie of vassalage. Because of Mircea's relationship with Sigismund, Vlad, his grandson and next in the line for succession, was sent at an early age to Sigismund's court. Vlad, as the heir to the throne of Wallachia, sought the protection of Sigismund in the defence against the Turks. Sigismund thus inducted Vlad in the Order of the Dragon, which granted him the grace of the Prince.

The Order was founded by the Holy Roman Emperor in 1387 with the character of a secret fraternal society. Like many other religious orders of knights, its objectives and duties were to protect the king and his family, to defend the empire, to spread the word of Catholicism, to protect children and widows, and, of course, to fight the infidel Turks. The reason for the secrecy of the Order seems to have been the undeclared ultimate aim to gain political supremacy in Europe for the House of Luxembourg.

In February 1431, Vlad was made a knight of the Order of the Dragon. Among the rules of the Order there were some that give us some interesting clues into the making of Dracula's legend. A new knight was required to attire himself in the following way: he had to wear two capes, one green (to symbolize the colour of a dragon), to be worn over red garments which represented the blood of the martyrs. The other cape was black, later adopted by Bram Stoker's Count Dracula, to be worn only on Fridays or on the occasion of a celebration. In addition, each member of the Order was required to wear a medallion with the insignia of the dragon artfully created by a master craftsman. The dragon was represented with two wings and four

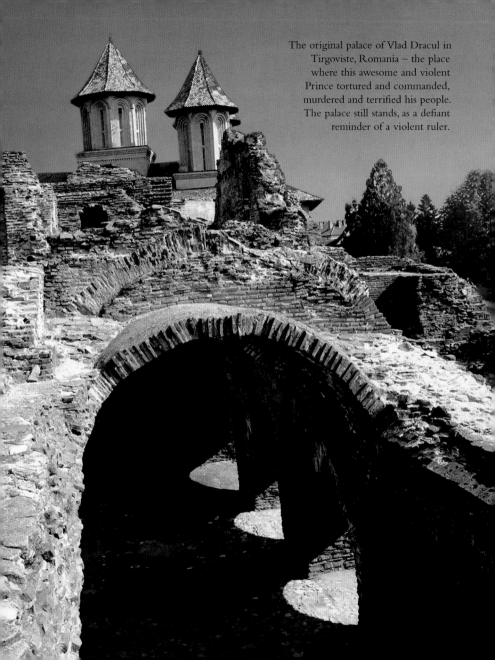

The original palace of Vlad Dracul in Tirgoviste, Romania – the place where this awesome and violent Prince tortured and commanded, murdered and terrified his people. The palace still stands, as a defiant reminder of a violent ruler.

paws out-stretched, with jaws half open, its tail curled around its head and its back cleft in two, hanging prostrate in front of a double cross. This symbolized the victory of Christ over the forces of darkness. The medallion had to be worn at all times until the member's death and it was to be placed in the coffin after death.

When Vlad returned to his native country, he was known as 'Dracul' by the landowning nobility, the boyars of Wallachia, as they recognized his honour as a Draconist, or member of the order of the Dragon (*draco* in Latin). However, the general population of Wallachia, unfamiliar with Vlad's knighthood, saw a dragon on his shield and on his coins, and called him 'Dracul' meaning 'devil'. In orthodox iconography, particularly those icons depicting St. George slaying the dragon, the dragon represented the devil. The word *drac* in Romanian, moreover, can either mean a dragon or a devil.

The entire family of Vlad came to be known to the general population and even in history books as Dracul. Vlad's son soon became known as 'Dracula' as the suffix '–a' simply means 'son of' in Romanian. This was the name adopted by Bram Stoker. Dracula was literally, then, the son of Dracul, or the one reborn from Dracul as we shall see. The bloody deeds in Dracula's career and the double meaning of his name contributed to the evil associated with him. Thus a legend was born.

As soon as Vlad was made a knight of the order of the Dragon, he swore allegiance to the Emperor and was given his official staff of office and declared Prince of Wallachia. However, Vlad's dreams of taking possession of the Wallachian throne did not materialize immediately. According to Wallachian rule, any son of the Prince, whether legitimate or not, could claim the throne as long as he was the eldest. While Vlad was away being educated at court, his half-brother, Alexandru Aldea, had seized the throne. The Emperor wished to continue his recognition of Alexandru as the Prince for political reasons and appointed Vlad, despite his new admission to the order, as military governor of Transylvania with the task of controlling the borders.

Vlad Dracul decided to establish his headquarters in the fortress of Sighisoara because of its central and strategic position. The hillside fort had unusually thick defensive walls one thousand metres long, made of stone and brick. It had recently been rebuilt to withstand even the strongest artillery the Turks could muster. In addition, there were 14 battlement-capped donjons (massive inner towers), each named after the guild that bore its cost (tailors, jewellers, furriers, butchers, goldsmiths and so on). The massive towers made the fortress impenetrable.

The early Princes of Romania shared with the Ottomans the harem system which made little distinction between legitimate wives and concubines. The only thing that really mattered in a candidate's suitability for the throne was that he was 'of royal male bone'. Vlad Dracul sired three legitimate sons. The second son, also called Vlad Dracul, was born in December 1431 and was to become world famous as Prince Dracula, the Impaler.

Vlad Dracul's main aim was to gain possession of what he considered his legitimate throne in Wallachia, even though it was still being occupied by his half-brother. In 1434, Sigismund saw that Alexandru's relationship with the Turks was too close for his liking, so he ordered Vlad to form an army of Transylvanian soldiers and to take possession of Wallachia. Vlad Dracul fought the Turks with his army in 1436 and took Tirgoviste, the capital of Wallachia, to become Prince with the sanction of the Emperor.

For young Dracula, life at his father's court was a wholly new experience. He was of eligible age for an apprenticeship into knighthood: he was taught swimming, fencing, jousting, archery, court etiquette and the more refined aspects of horsemanship. He was also introduced to political science, the principles of which were in essence Machiavellian. It was believed at the time that it was much better for a prince to be feared than to be loved; this way of thinking must have strongly moulded Dracula's personality.

Local tradition has it that the young Dracula was almost morbidly fascinated from a very early age by criminals being led from jail to the Jeweller's Donjon, where they would be executed by hanging.

Die facht sich an gar ein graussem
liche erschrockenliche hystorien von dem wilden reürich.
Dracole wayde. Wie er die leüt gespißt hat. vnd geprauten.
vnd mit den haübtern yn einem kessel gesoten. vn wie er die
leüt geschunden hat vn zerhacken lassen als ein kraut. Jtez
er hat auch den mütern ire kind gepraten vnd sy haben müs-
sen selber essen. Vnd vil andere erschrockenliche ding die in
dissem Tractat geschriben stend. Vnd in welchem land er
geregirt hat.

Vlad Dracul's tortures and methods of execution were the most ghastly
anyone has ever devised.

Sigismund, King of Luxembourg and patron and protector of the Dracul
family, died in 1437, leaving Wallachia and its ruling family exposed to the
growing assaults and strength of the Turks. Shortly after Sigismund's death,
Vlad Dracul had no option but to sign a pact of alliance with Sultan Murad
II of Turkey. It seems that Vlad Dracul used to accompany Murad II on
frequent raids of Transylvania, during which killing, pillaging and burning of
villages occurred. This undoubtedly built the legend of the bloodthirsty
nature of the Dracula family.

After the death of his father, young Dracula was held a captive prisoner of
the Turks, where he served as an officer in the army. During this time he had
ample opportunity to learn all the methods of torture employed by Turkish

forces on prisoners of war. The Koran, for instance, prescribed that sexual initiation between two men should be started by the seducer wounding the would-be lover with his sword before intercourse. Impalement of prisoners seems also to have been a customary form of punishment.

Despite all the learning and experience Dracula accumulated in the Turkish army, he was still a prisoner of the Sultan and longed to seize the throne of Wallachia in much the same way as his father, Vlad Dracul, had done before him. Dracula thus decided to flee the court of the Turkish Sultan and to find refuge in Moldavia, a neighbouring state of Wallachia, where he hoped to find protection and to be able to put together an army to put him on the Wallachian throne. After a few adventures and failed attempts, Dracula finally became the official prince of Wallachia in 1456, barely 25 years of age.

The beginning of his reign was hailed by the passing of a comet over Europe, and astrologers of the time generally regarded this as a celestial sign, an omen of bad luck and a prelude to earthquakes, illnesses, plagues, wars and other numerous catastrophes. Dracula, on the other hand, saw it as a fateful start to his dominance of Wallachia and inscribed the comet on one side of his coins, the other bearing the Wallachian eagle.

Dracula established his main residence at Tirgoviste, which was not only the seat of power, but also the centre of the nation's social and cultural life. Dracula's palace, in today's standards, was of modest proportions. It was dominated by the watchtower he had built from which he could survey the countryside and keep look out for an impending attack from the Turks, and from which he could also observe the daily slaughtering he ordered in the courtyard below. The Chindia Watchtower still stands today, an important landmark on the vampire trail. Next to the winecellars, storage rooms and the baths in the palace, there can still be seen numerous torture chambers where he kept his dying prisoners.

The boyars were the noble landowning families and they formed, by tradition, the council of Wallachia on which even the Prince had ultimately to depend for orders and matters of administration and justice. The boyars, therefore, held even more power than the ruler, and it was in their interest to elect the weakest possible prince, one who was not likely to intervene in their decision making. The central power was thus unstable, and there had been a rapid succession of princes, each only reigning for just two years. Dracula was soon to change the political situation dramatically and overthrow the power of the boyars in favour of a more centralized system which he headed with an iron fist. Dracula also sought personal revenge against the boyars, since they had killed one of his brothers by burying him alive, a crime he could not forgive.

An ancient Romanian chronicle cites the events that took place in the spring of 1457,

> He (Dracula) had found out that the boyars of Tirgoviste had buried one of his brothers alive. In order to know the truth, he searched for his brother in the grave and found him lying face downwards. So when Easter day came, while all the citizens were feasting and the young ones were dancing, he surrounded them … led them together with their wives and their children, just as they were dressed up for Easter, to Poenari (site of the famous castle Dracula), where they were put to work until their clothes were torn and they were left naked.

Popular tradition held that Dracula first impaled the children and the wives in the courtyard of his palace, and then the men were put in chains and led to a location known as the Source of the River, a journey that took two days. Here he ordered them to reconstruct the ancient castle which was in ruins. Dracula had given orders to the villagers living close to the castle to build brick ovens and lime kilns. The boyars, under constant threat of the whip of Dracula's guards, formed a chain from the villages where the bricks were being manufactured, to the walls of the castle which they laboriously rebuilt.

Local folklore claims that inside the rebuilt castle there is a secret passage that leads deep under the mountains, reputedly used by Dracula for his mysterious practices. Even today in the superstitious minds of the local peasants, there is a strong belief in a 'Dracula-curse' associated with this evil place where so many souls suffered. They say that a golden flame sometimes lights up in the sky at night, reflected by the ill-obtained treasure that Dracula extracted from the boyars, and that no one should try to find the treasure lest he succumb to the terrible curse.

To replace the boyars, Dracula created his own nobility, much in the same fashion as the early Neapolitan mafia, formed largely by men of plebeian origin. Breaking the tradition by which the lands and riches confiscated from a boyar were given to another nobleman from the same privileged class, Dracula gave them instead to this mass of men. They owed their power to his will entirely and due to their ruthless and vested interest in the survival of his regime, they carried out the duties allotted to them by the dreaded Vlad with the violence the Prince intended when he ordered them.

The joy in his own power, however, not only drove Dracula to reduce the class of boyars to little more than obedient servants, but also to administer heavy punishment to whomever dared to offend him, intentionally or not. The following is a contemporary account describing an Italian diplomatic delegation which had gone to Wallachia from Genoa.

> *I have found that some Italians came as ambassadors to his court. As they came to him they took off their hats and hoods facing the prince. Under the hat, each of them wore a coif or a little skullcap that he did not take off, as is the habit among Italians. Dracula then asked them for an explanation of why they had only taken their hats off, leaving their skullcaps on their heads. To which they answered. "This is our custom. We are not obliged to take our skullcaps off under any circumstances, even an audience with the sultan or the Holy Roman Emperor." Dracula then said. "In all fairness, I want to strengthen and*

Dracula established his main residence at Tirgoviste, which was not only the seat of power, but also the centre of the nation's social and cultural life.

recognize your customs." They thanked him, bowing to him; and added. "Sire we shall always serve you with your interests if you show us such goodness, and we shall praise your greatness everywhere." Then in a deliberate manner this tyrant and killer did the following: he took some big iron nails and planted them in a circle in the head of each ambassador. "'Believe me," he said while his attendants nailed the skullcaps on the heads of the envoys, "this is the manner in which I will strengthen your custom."

It is said that to see for himself how the work on the land of his peasant people was progressing, Vlad Dracul the younger roamed across the country-side in disguise, particularly at night. He wanted to know how the peasants lived, how well and how much they worked, and what they were thinking about. Sometimes he would stop at individual peasant houses and ask all manner of questions. This particular trait was to be adopted by the romantic vampire as well: he showed concern towards his villagers not because they farmed his land profitably, but rather because they represented a source of fresh blood. Both the fictional and the historical Dracula seem to share the role of monster and protector at once, gripping the populace within a painful and unbreakable bond.

The following ballad testifies to the methods imposed by the Prince on the peasants of this beleaguered land.

One day Dracula met a peasant who was wearing too short a shirt. One could also notice his homespun peasant trousers, which were stuck to his legs, and one could make out the sides of his thighs. When he saw him dressed in this manner, Dracula immediately ordered him to be brought to court. "Are you married?" he enquired. "Yes, I am, Your Highness." "Your wife is assuredly the kind who remains idle. How is it possible that your shirt does not cover the calf of your leg? She is not worthy of living in my realm. May she perish!" "Beg forgiveness, my lord, but I am satisfied with her. She never leaves home and she is honest." "You will be more satisfied with another since you are a decent and hardworking man." Two of Dracula's men had in the meantime brought the wretched woman to him, and she was immediately impaled. Then bringing

The watchtower of Vlad Dracul's palace in Tirgoviste, from where the dreaded Prince watched his subjects impaled and tortured in the courtyard. What souls still wander hereabouts, still reliving the horrors of their lives?

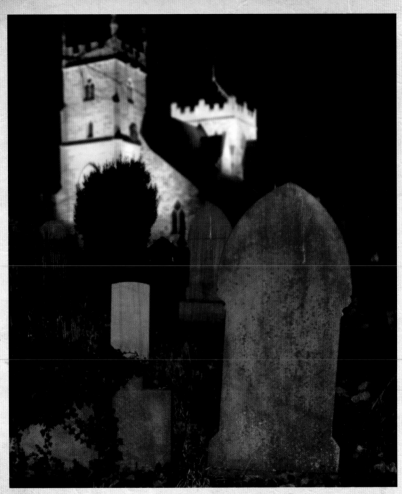

Close by Vlad Dracul's castle lie the gravestones of those he murdered and tortured, standing in rows within a dark wood, the souls perhaps still haunting one of the most terrible scenes of history.

another woman, he gave her away to be married to the peasant widower. Dracula, however, was careful to show the new wife what had happened to her predecessor and explain to her the reasons why she had incurred the princely wrath. Consequently, the new wife worked so hard she had no time to eat. She placed the bread on one shoulder, the salt on another, and worked in this fashion. She tried hard to give greater satisfaction to her new husband than the first wife not to incur the curse of Dracula.

Prince Dracula punished the parasites of society, the beggars and vagabonds, extremely harshly and cruelly to set an example for the rest of the population so that they may work hard and not revolt against his rule. There is one account of this that is so well known that it has, through the centuries, been translated in several languages: German, Russian and Romanian. In this example, drawn from the Romanian version, Dracula purges Wallachia of the beggars, the sick and the poor.

Having invited the old, the ill, the lame, the poor, the blind and the vagabonds to a large dining hall in Tirgoviste, Dracula ordered that a feast be prepared for them. On the appointed day, Tirgoviste groaned under the weight of the large number of beggars who had come. The prince's servants passed out a batch of clothes to each one, then they led the beggars to a large mansion where tables had been set. The beggars marvelled at the prince's generosity, and they spoke among themselves, "Truly it is a prince's kind of grace." Then they started eating. And what do you think they saw before them: a meal such as one would find on the prince's own table: wines and all the finest delicacies to fill their bellies. The beggars had a feast that became legendary. They ate and drank greedily and most of them were inebriated. As they became unable to communicate with one another, and became incoherent, they were suddenly faced with fire and smoke on all sides. The prince had ordered his servants to set the house on fire. They rushed to the doors to get out, but the doors were locked. The fire burned on. The flames rose high like dancing dragons. Shouts, shrieks and moans arose from the lips of all the poor enclosed there. But why should a fire be moved by the entreaties of men? They fell upon each other.

They embraced each other. They sought help, but there was no human ear left to listen to them. They began to twist in the torments of the fire that was destroying them. The fire stifled some, the embers reduced others to ashes, the flames grilled most of them. When the fire naturally abated, there was no trace of any living soul.

So great was the fear of impalement that throughout Dracula's reign, theft and other crimes completely disappeared. It was not so much the virtue of the Machiavellian prince, but rather his tortured mind that imposed this clean order. The memory of his cruelty remains stamped in the tales drawn from Romanian folklore.

If any wife had an affair outside of marriage, Dracula ordered her sexual organs cut. She was then skinned alive and exposed in her skinless flesh in the public square, her skin hanging separately from a pole or placed on a table in the middle of the marketplace. The same punishment was applied to maidens who did not keep their virginity, and also to unchaste widows. For lesser offenses, Dracula was known to have the nipple of a woman's breast cut off. He also had a red-hot iron stake shoved into a woman's vagina, making the instrument penetrate her entrails and emerge from her mouth. He then had the woman tied to a pole naked and left her exposed there until the flesh fell from the body, and the bones detached themselves from their sockets.

Dracula's Death, Dracula's Birth

Little is known of Dracul's place of burial. Ancient Romanian chronicles state that he was buried at Snagov in an ancient monastery that Dracul had helped to rebuild while he was still alive. The monastery still stands to this day, albeit in ruins, on an island in the middle of a tranquil lake. In the superstitious imaginations of the people of Snagov, the terrible figure of the Impaler is still believed to haunt the grounds surrounding the small and perhaps deceptively peaceful church.

Surrounding the lake on all sides is the dense forest of Vlasia. The island of Snagov commands an excellent view and is furthermore protected on all sides by water. Even in winter, it is said, when the lake is completely frozen, a cannon shot from the island could break up the ice and thus drown any approaching enemies. A popular folklore tradition states that the monastery was rebuilt by Dracul in the form of a fortress, and that the treasures his accomplices had stolen from the boyars were kept within the holy walls; the monks, however, fearful of tempting the Turks with the treasures, threw them into the lake where they still lie today.

Other peasant narratives tell of Dracul's crimes on the island. It is believed that he kept the monastery as a prison and that he tortured many in its cells. The recent discovery of decapitated skeletons, with the skulls placed alongside the pierced bodies, seems to give foundation to this legend which claims that the Prince carried out his impalements even here. Although archaeologists have completed a series of excavations at Snagov, the remains of Prince Dracul have not yet been found. There is an ancient legend, however, that tells of a fearsome devil's school in the mountains, mentioned even by Bram Stoker in his novel, which reputedly the Draculs attended.

> They (the Draculs) learned the secrets in the Scholomance, amongst the mountains over Lake Hermannstadt, where the devil claims the tenth scholar as his due.

There is further evidence of the school from Western chroniclers:

> … a school supposed to exist somewhere in the heart of the mountains, and where all the secrets of nature, the language of animals, and all imaginable magic spells and charms are taught by the devil in person. Only ten scholars are admitted at a time, and when the course of learning has expired and nine of them are released to return to their homes, the tenth scholar is detained by the devil as payment, and mounted upon an Ismeju (the correct Romanian spelling of the word is Zmcu, meaning dragon) he becomes henceforth the devil's aide-de-camp. …A small lake, immeasurably deep, lying high up among the mountains of Hermannstadt, is supposed to be the cauldron where is brewed the thunder, and in fair weather the dragon sleeps beneath the water.

"...a school supposed to exist somewhere in the heart of the mountains, and where all the secrets of nature, the language of animals, and all imaginable magic spells and charms are taught by the devil in person."

The word 'Scholomance' derives from the Romanian *solomari*, meaning the 'students of alchemy.' It is a corruption of the word Solomon, the wise judge in the Bible, whom legend turned into an alchemist. Since legendary places are kept secret, or their true location is hidden with the name of a different town, it may be that Dracula was buried at the secret school of Hermannstadt, or that the secret school was situated at Snagov. The monks of Snagov explain that even today the island is a remote and isolated place and that they have to store away supplies in autumn in preparation for the harsh winter that cuts them off from the outside world. Snagov, moreover, was an ancient place of learning. May it be that imagination confused the two places, intertwining each of the legends to form a third which describes where Dracula was buried and how he came about his magical practices? The credence that Dracul attended the Scholomance school would explain his passage from the pages of history books to become a fictional, supernatural character.

It is said that the most important day of the year for Romanian peasants, and indeed for much of the old Germanic and eastern European people, is St. George's Day, on the 23rd of April. On the night of St. George's Day many occult meetings take place at night in lonely caverns or within ruined walls. On this night all the rituals which celebrate the witches' Sabbath are put into practice. This same night is also said to be the best for finding treasures. On the night of St. George's day all the treasures begin to burn, to bloom in the bosom of the earth, and the light they give forth, described as a bluish flame resembling the colour of burning wine spirit, serves to guide mortals to their place of concealment. It may be that on this night a favoured mortal searching for Prince Dracula might see a light emanating from the waters of the lake where his treasure is drowned… for the dragon, Dracula's symbol, favours that night for the search.

But most strange of all the legends and stories surrounding Vlad Dracul is that he returned to his home two hundred years later and was seen and witnessed by many as the son of the same family, born into different times. His appearance was similar to the depictions of his dreaded great-great-great grandfather, though he was reported to be more noble and less obviously violent in his ways. The times into which he returned were more peaceful times and the new Prince Dracula fitted in well. These same stories uphold that the Prince of Darkness never died and his coffin has never been found because he carries it with him to this day.

If we analyze the nature and extent of the crimes committed by Prince Dracula during his reign, we might draw the conclusion that he was one of the greatest and cruelest psychopaths in history. It has been estimated that his victims range in number from a minimum of 40,000 to a maximum of 100,000, nearly a fifth of the total population of Wallachia, which had approximately half a million inhabitants.

Stakes stood permanently prepared in his courtyard at Tirgoviste and in various strategic places, such as public squares and marketplaces. It is said that the stakes were carefully rounded and bathed in oil so that the organs of the victims should not be pierced by a fatal wound immediately. Dracula was said to oversee the legs of his victims being tied to two horse. He would personally whip both horses so that they would go running in different directions, while his attendants held the body and the stake on which it was impaled firmly in place. Some impalements, however, were not from the buttocks up, but from the navel, the heart, the stomach and the chest.

Dracula did not by any means restrict himself to impalement, however, but it is this gruesome Eastern practice of driving a wooden stake through the heart or a vital part of the body which contributed to the belief that a vampire can only be killed in this way. It may be that the poor souls who suffered at the hands of Dracula, the Prince of Darkness, are still seeking revenge and inspire, unconsciously, the vampire hunter to administer the same punishment to any members of the Dracula clan. It is true that Dracula not only killed men, but also children, the elderly and women. Such crimes are not easily forgotten.

Dracula also decapitated his victims, cut off noses, ears, sexual organs and limbs; he nailed hats to heads; he blinded, strangled, hanged, burned, boiled, skinned, roasted, hacked and buried alive. It is also suspected that he practiced cannibalism, eating the limbs of those he killed, and drinking their blood. It can be proved that he forced others to eat human flesh and that he used to smear prisoners' soles with salt and honey and allowed animals to lick them for an indefinite period of suffering.

To conclude, stories of the madness that had taken possession of Prince Dracula and drove him to commit the worst crimes history had ever experienced were spread by monks and travellers from Wallachia to central Europe. Here, among a cultured and less barbaric population who prided itself in having attained the 'renaissance' of man, but nevertheless was hungry for tales of horror of far-away places such as Wallachia, the legend of Dracula grew out of all proportion. The monster of history became alive in the pages of the earliest horror stories; some of his real traits, such as the almost physical pleasure that pain and torture produced in him, the thirst for blood, and his noble origins, were kept intact and can be found, unchanged, in modem vampire stories. Other traits, such as a vampire's long canine teeth, his hypnotic stare, and his immortality, were added to these tales partly by the fervid imagination that still quivered in the memory of medieval horror stories and superstitions, and partly by evidence, which was springing up all over Europe, that blood-drinking creatures really did exist.

Moreover, Prince Dracula was not, according to all accounts, just a psychopath and a man suffering from sexual impotence who thrilled in seeing the stake being driven through the genitals of his victims. There are a few mysteries that lead the adventurous reader from the gruesome to the supernatural and these mostly surround his death, his coffin that was never found, and a connection between his death and an ancient school of occult learning, whose existence has been kept secret for centuries. And it is here that we begin to see the final connection between the death of Prince Vlad Dracul and the birth of his reborn son The Prince of Darkness, Dracula himself.

Chapter 5

Family of
Vampires

True vampires long for a quiet existence, to be lived in the great halls of castles hidden amid the Carpathian mountains, or in dark and thick forests. Anonymity is the very tool of survival for a vampire since, as soon as his or her existence is discovered, it is at great risk. The endless, slow monotony is interrupted only by the thirst for blood which compels these creatures to look for a victim among mortals.

There are, however, a few exceptions, as there are in all natural and super-natural things. Some vampires bathe in the limelight and in high society: their game of hide-and-seek with victims and vampire hunters providing a pleas-ant diversion to their eternity. The titillation and excitement of being swifter in movement, governed by laws outside those of the human world and to possess a unique knowledge of history by direct experience over centuries. With the endowment of hypnotic powers to paralyze victims, the power to become invisible, to be, in other words, quite different from us mortals, all this must be an amusing distraction when moving amid human circles. As the few vampires that lead this kind of existence are so different from humans, they are bound to become the centre of attention wherever they go. Thus, a few vampires have become very famous, and tales surrounding these precious few have been told countless times, for they always afford great pleasure. Their success is due not only to the fact that it is the story of a supernatural, monstrous, and yet fascinating creature, but also because these vampires move in an absolutely normal milieu – a contemporary setting. Evil is perhaps still more terrifying when met in a recognizable world, rather than in a remote and foreign atmosphere. Take Lord Ruthven, for example...

Lord Ruthven

Lord Ruthven is an English vampire, living in London, the city where he was born. The winter in London is marked by a round of parties held by leading socialites, and Lord Ruthven, a true nobleman, is often invited more for his singularities than for his blue-blooded rank. He spends his summers abroad, preferably in Greece where there are still so many remote areas he can visit, and where he can remain alone and undisturbed.

Lord Ruthven is cool by nature and seldom displays his wit and supernatural skills. Apparently, only the laughter of the very fair attracts him. His face, although very handsome, is always darkened by a deadly hue and never gains a warmer tint. This does not seem to put off the hunters of notoriety who, appreciating his absolute aristocratic values, often seek to obtain his affection. He has, moreover, the reputation of a winning tongue, and it is perhaps for this reason that every good hostess seeks to have him on her list of guests.

It is rumoured that Lord Ruthven possesses irresistible powers of seduction as well as having licentious habits which make him dangerous to beautiful hostesses. To enhance his own gratification after the seduction, Lord Ruthven requires that his companion in sin be hurled from the pinnacle of virtue to the very lowest abyss of infamy and degradation. His preference lies with inexperienced young girls of the noble classes,

Robert Polidori wrote his experiences as fiction, detailing the life of Lord Ruthven.

although he has been known to entertain the favours of mature, and even married, women. When asked what his intentions are in regard to the inexperienced girls, he answers that they are such as he supposes all would have upon such an occasion. When asked whether he would marry the girl, after having taken her virtue, he answers with a cruel laugh. Women who were previously beautiful and animated become dispirited and lifeless after a shortlived relationship with Lord Ruthven. Others have become mad with passion, and after their affair with him the only thing they wish for is death.

Lord Ruthven's passion seems to be aroused beyond measure when he can take a girl loved by another, especially if it is a man who considers the nobleman as a friend. Lord Ruthven himself claims to have no friends, but may occasionally act as though he favours one or other of his companions, his generosity increasing if he spies a pretty, innocent girl accompanying them. If the man tries to stop him from taking possession of the girl, Lord Ruthven will attack with a strength that can best be described as a superhuman force.

Many a hurt lover has attempted to murder Lord Ruthven, and some have even succeeded, or thought they had. In one instance, servants placed the dead body of the lord on top of a mountain, so that it might be exposed to the first cold ray of the moon that rose after his death, his fondest wish. However, when his adversary climbed the mountain the next day he found no trace of the body, nor of the clothes. The conclusion was that the servants had stolen the beautiful clothes of the nobleman and buried the corpse so that no one would find out. Lord Ruthven had in fact murdered his adversary's lover, although the latter did not know of the event, as it had occurred during the night and there was yet no suspicion of vampirism. Imagine then the horror that seized him when, on his return to London, he saw Lord Ruthven partying again amid elegant circles of admirers, gaining the favours of his own sister, the only friend left to him. The story ends with the man being so distraught by the loss first of his beloved and second his sister that he dies of pain and madness, whilst Lord Ruthven has quenched his vampire thirst on two beautiful young women.

Varney the Vampire

Varney is a lurid creature who loves to wake up beautiful young women by scratching with his talons at the window-panes of their bedrooms while they sleep, imitating with his nails the noise of hail beating against the glass, for his preference is to attack on stormy nights.

His face is perfectly white and perfectly blood-less. His eyes look like polished tin and when he draws back his lips, fearful teeth are displayed, projecting like those of some wild animal, hideous and glaringly white and fang-like. His nails literally hang from the ends of his fingers, and he likes to clatter them together, producing a hair-raising sound which paralyzes the victims. His awful, metallic-looking eyes are as hypnotic as those of a great serpent; his strength can only be described as superhuman.

Varney enjoys most the pleasures of violating a young woman's beautifully rounded body, employing his hideous manliness while making a dreadful sucking noise, drinking blood from the side of his victim's neck. After feeding, his face becomes hideously flushed and his eyes have a savage and remarkable luster. Whereas before they shone like metal, after the attack they are ten times brighter and flashes of light seem to dart from them. Varney can be recognized from the dreadful howling that issues from his throat.

The Knight Azzo

The Knight Azzo lives at Castle Klatka, which is situated in the Carpathian Mountains, in Romania. The castle, reputed to have been abandoned by humans but haunted for centuries, stands within the lands belonging to the Knight of Fahnenberg, the descendent of a noble Austrian family. The title of the Fahnenberg family is inherited along with the lands and property both in Austria and abroad. Every time the new Knight of Fahnenberg visits his castle in Romania, he meets the strange and exotic Knight Azzo, who has been living there and roaming the wild forests around the castle for hundreds of years.

The Knight Azzo appears to be a man of about 40, tall and extremely thin. His features are bold and daring, although his expression is not in the least benevolent. There is great contempt and sarcasm in his cold eyes, and his glances are so piercing that no one can endure his stare for long. His complexion is even more peculiar than his eyes: it is neither pale nor yellow, but rather grey, like that of an Indian who has been suffering long from fever. His complexion is rendered even more remarkable by the blackness of his beard and short-cropped hair.

He dresses in the style of a knight, but his clothes are old-fashioned and neglected. There are great spots of rust on the collar and breast-plate of his armour. He carries a dagger and a sword, as do all proper knights.

Although Knight Azzo accepts supper invitations from his neighbours, the Knight of Fahnenberg and his family, he never eats, claiming that his digestion is quite unused to solid food and that he lives entirely on liquids.

He likes to be addressed as Azzo von Klatka by those he entertains with his opinions on existential matters. He is drawn most readily into conversations with or in the presence of unmarried, beautiful young ladies, while he is likely to be rude, cold, sarcastic and insulting to the chosen lady's fiance or any young man who might dare to challenge his wit or strength.

The Knight Azzo loves everything that is peculiar and uncommon; he talks to wolves, and even these fierce beasts obey him and become like docile lambs in his presence. He claims that all things are alike: life and death, this side of the grave and the other, have more resemblance, in his view, than we might otherwise imagine. He amuses himself with hunting and has been known to spend many a moonless night roaming in the dark forest and marshland surrounding Castle Klatka. He also loves to ride on a horse that never tires in the pale moonlight over hills and dales, through wide, open forests and remote woodlands.

The Knight does not receive or see anyone unless the moon is shining brightly. With strangers he is coldly polite and tends to speak with few words. But from his way of talking, one can detect a deep hatred, a cold detestation of all mankind, with the exception of fair young ladies.

Carmilla

Carmilla is an anagram of the true name of Mircalla, Countess Karnstein. She has appeared, throughout the centuries, under many names, all anagrams of the original: Millarca and Carmilla are two of the most famous of her incarnations.

The features of the Countess, however, have remained unaltered in all the centuries since her death. She appears as a young girl, of not even 20 years of age, and of magnificent beauty. She is above average height for a woman, slender and wonderfully graceful; her movements are languid, *very* languid, and her large eyes never seem to blink and rest upon objects for long periods of time, unmoved in their gaze. Her complexion is rich and brilliant; her features small and beautifully formed; her eyes large, dark and lustrous. Seldom has anyone seen such hair, so magnificently thick and long when it falls about her shoulders. It is exquisitely fine and soft, and in colour a rich, very dark brown, with flecks of gold in it.

Carmilla speaks in a sweet low voice and loves to chat and entertain with harmless, sweet gossip. Her beauty, grace, manners and her conversation are so exquisite that she is invited to countless society balls.

Little is known about her, since she exercises an alert reserve when asked about her mother, family, origins, her life, her plans and everything that surrounds her. She claims that her mother has made her promise not to reveal anything to anyone although, in order not to hurt her friends, she

The female vampiress gained much ground during the nineteenth century – from being merely a slave of male vampires to being a rabid killer in her own right. Above, Maila Nurmi, who created the camp 1950s character Vampira.

Carmilla is a very sensuous creature; she falls utterly, desperately in love with a girl and wishes for nothing but to die with her. She kisses her cheek, draws breath very near her neck, and holds the girl's hands tight against her own heart.

constantly promises them that in good time she will tell all. She admits to only three things: first, her name is Carmilla, or any anagrammatical variation of it; second, her family is very ancient and noble; and third, her home lies in the direction of the west.

Carmilla invariably appears in the company of her mother and strikes up an acquaintance with a lovely girl of her own age, who generally lives alone with her father in some remote chateau. Young people, especially young girls, like and love on impulse, and it is endearing for their fathers to see their own daughter find such pleasure and delight in the company of such a beautiful and noble girl. Carmilla's mother, in the stories they concoct together, is called away on urgent and vital business, leaving her daughter in the hands of the father, who readily promises to look after her until the older Countess returns, several months later. Carmilla, according to her mother, cannot travel the far distances required, as she is in delicate health and somewhat nervous. Because of Carmilla's beauty and her sincere friendship with his daughter, the father always consents gladly to the Countess's will, since he can see nothing but delight and pleasure coming into his lonely home with the presence of Carmilla to warm their hearts.

Carmilla's habits seem odd, especially so to rustic people. She does not come down from her room until very late, usually well into the afternoon. She then takes a cup of chocolate, but eats nothing. And whenever she goes out for a walk she seems, almost immediately, to feel exhausted and must either return to the castle or sit to rest on one of the garden benches. She is also in the habit of locking all the rooms of her living quarters at night, claiming that some robbers broke into her room many years before and she has been terrified ever since of it occurring again. However, local gossip says that she has been seen wandering about in the nearby forest at night, like a soul without repose.

Carmilla loathes funeral processions, and whenever she sees one she has a fit of rage, her face turning livid, her body shaking violently, and her fists becoming tightly clenched. This, however, only lasts a few moments until she regains possession of herself and behaves as if nothing had happened.

Carmilla is a very sensuous creature; she falls utterly, desperately in love with a girl and wishes for nothing but to die with her. She kisses her cheek, draws breath very near her neck, and holds the girl's hands tight against her own heart. This is a description of Carmilla's ardour from the hand of one of her victims:

> *Sometimes, after an hour of apathy, my strange and beautiful companion would take my hand and hold it with a fond pressure, renewed again and again; blushing softly, gazing in my face with languid and burning eyes, and breathing so fast that her dress rose and fell with the tumultuous respiration. It was like the ardour of a lover; it embarrassed me; it was hateful and yet overpowering; and with gloating eyes she drew me to her, and her hot lips travelled along my cheek in kisses; and she would whisper, almost in sobs, "You are mine, you shall be mine, and you and I are one forever." Then she has thrown herself back in her chair, with her small hands over her eyes, leaving me trembling.*

Almost as soon as Carmilla settles in a region, there appear to be a number of medically inexplicable deaths; women who die suddenly of a 24-hour illness. At the same time, her friend and companion, Carmilla's much cherished and loved victim, receives nightly visits from what appears to be a large, black and sinister cat, pacing back and forth in the bedroom with the restlessness of a caged beast. As the room grows darker and darker, the cat springs onto the bed and the victim feels a stinging pain, as if two large needles had darted, a little apart, deep into her breast. Carmilla has in fact two abilities: she can transform herself into a large black cat and she can make herself invisible.

The true story of Mircalla, Countess of Karnstein, is a sad and singular one. While still alive, in the year 1698, she was attacked by a vampire and thus became one herself. An ancestor of Baron Vordenburg, the man who eventually succeeded in killing her centuries later, held the Countess as his idol and loved her greatly. Even though he suspected her of vampirism, his greatest horror was that her beautiful remains would be profaned by the outrage of a posthumous execution, as is customary with suspected vampires. The Baron had left a curious paper which proved that a vampire, on being killed again, is projected into a far more horrible life, evidence which he had found in ancient books of the occult. Wishing to spare his beloved Mircalla from such

"You are mine, you shall be mine, and you and I are one forever."

a horrid fate, he journeyed to the castle of the Karnsteins and pretended to remove her remains. He changed the position of her grave, hiding it with plants so that it would remain undiscovered. Upon his death, however, he realized what he had done and left a diary in which he had made sketches and notes to guide future vampire hunters to the spot where the grave had been placed. The diary also contained a detailed confession of the deception that he had practiced.

The village surrounding Castle Karnstein had been abandoned after the death of the Countess, and the descendants of those who had served the Countess during her life of course had taken it for granted that she had been killed again as a vampire. As this wasn't true, the beautiful Carmilla had continued to kill hundreds of women until her coffin was found, a stake was driven through her heart, and her remains were burned and thrown into the waters of the nearby river. Nothing is known about who the distinguished lady who claimed to be Carmilla's mother might have been.

A scene from Phil Claydon's film *Lesbian Vampire Killers* (2009), with the actress Silvia Colloca as Carmilla. The film is a tongue-in-cheek homage to the classic Hammer Horror films.

Julia Stone

Julia Stone lives in a room at the top of an ancient tower which still stands in the Ashdown Forest in the south of England. A portrait of her hangs in the room; it depicts an old, withered, white-haired woman. The picture shows an evident feebleness in her body, but a dreadful exuberance and vitality shine through the old flesh, an exuberance which is wholly malign. She demonstrates a vitality which foams and froths with unimaginable evil. Evil beams from the narrow, leering eyes, and a wicked laughter comes from her demon-like mouth. Her whole face contains some secret and appalling mirth. The hands, clasped together on the knee, seem to shake with suppressed and nameless glee. The signature on the painting, on the bottom left-hand corner, reads 'Julia Stone by Julia Stone'.

No one can remove the painting from the room in the tower. To begin with, it is so heavy that even three strongly built men cannot lift it off its hook. The painting, furthermore, cuts the hands and limbs of all those who attempt to remove it from its place and, even though the cuts are never visible, there is considerable bleeding. Visitors to the house who are unlucky enough to be forced by circumstance to sleep in the room at the top of the tower, are so frightened by the portrait of Julia Stone that they whole heartedly wish it to be removed, despite all the difficulties.

Julia Stone is said to appear at night, dressed in a clinging white garment, spotted and stained with mould. She attacks her victims, usually men, by pinning them down to the bed with her superhuman strength and sucking the blood from the side of the neck. Whenever she appears, there is a foul smell pervading the room, and her portrait hangs back on its hook as if it had never been removed.

Local records, which can be found in the church nearby, tell of an attempt that was made three times, many years ago, to bury the body of a certain woman who had committed suicide. On each occasion the coffin was found again protruding from the ground a few days later. After the third attempt, to avoid causing distress to the local community, the body was buried elsewhere in unconsecrated ground. The chosen spot for the reburial was just outside the iron gate of the garden that belonged to the house where this woman had lived. She had committed suicide in the room at the top of the tower in that same house. Her name was Julia Stone.

The Girl with the Hungry Eyes

This girl is a top model in the United States. But she is unlike any other. She is unnatural. She is morbid. And she is unholy.

The girl is the Face, the Body, and the Look of America, but no one knows anything about her, where she came from, where she lives, what she does, who she is, or even what her name is. She has never been drawn, nor painted. All her portraits have been copied from photographs. Neither has she ever been interviewed before now.

No one ever sees her, except one photographer who is making more money out of her than he ever dreamed of.

The girl has skinny arms, a thin neck and a slightly gaunt, almost prim face. She has a tumbling mass of dark hair and, peeping from under it, the hungriest eyes in the world. Her eyes are the reason why she is displayed all over the fashion magazine covers; the hunger in them is all sex, but at the same time something more than sex. Everyone has been wait-

Christina Fulton was *The Girl with the Hungry Eyes* in the Jon Jacobs film (1995).

ing for a model with this image: something more than sex. The girl has worked for only two photographers and has never given her name, telephone number or address to anyone. She arrives for work always on time, she is never tired, and she forbids the photographers to follow her out of the studio or so much as watch her leaving the building from the window, threatening that if they do so, they will have to hire another model.

There is a theory, conjured up by one of the photographers, that could explain the success of the girl. Suppose the desires of millions of people focused on one telepathic person. Say a girl. They shape her in their image. Imagine her knowing the hidden hunger of millions of men. Imagine her seeing deeper into that hunger than the people that are experiencing it, seeing the hatred and the wish for death behind their lust. Imagine her shaping herself in the image that they project on her, yet keeping herself as aloof as marble. Yet imagine the hunger she might feel in answer to their hunger. This is how the girl appears to the photographer, this is what he believes people feel when looking into her hungry eyes.

The first photographer ever to take a picture of her, and to make her famous, was the only one who eventually came to know her truth. He felt dizzy in the studio whenever she was there, attracted and strangely repelled by her presence at the same time. As the fame of the girl began to increase, the photographer looked through all the newspapers each morning to see how many of his photographs of her had been published. As he scanned the pages of the newspapers, however, he noticed that every week there had been murders in the city for which the police could find no explanation. The manner of killing was completely unknown and the police were baffled by the murders.

The photographer was hypnotized by the girl. He made a pass at her and she refused him with a smile. In the manner of men, there were many other passes, fewer smiles and more refusals. He eventually decided to follow her, risking his fame in attempting to find out more about her. He saw that she waited by the side of the curb until a car, driven by a young man, picked her up. They drove off together into the night. That evening, the photographer got drunk. The morning after, he saw the face of the young man in the paper: he had been murdered.

The photographer then decided to risk it all and to walk down the stairs with the girl on his arm after work. She asked him whether he knew what he was doing. He said he did. They went walking in the park, she was very quiet and eventually sat down on the grass, pulling him towards her. He started fumbling with her blouse but she pushed him off saying she did not want that.

What she wanted was this:

I want you. I want your high spots. I want everything that's made you happy and everything that's hurt you bad. I want your first girl. I want that shiny bicycle. I want that licking. I want that pinhole camera. I want your mother's death. I want the blue sky filled with stars. I want your blood on the cobble-stones. I want Mildred's mouth. I want the first picture you sold. I want the lights of Chicago. I want the gin. I want Gwen's hands. I want your wanting me. I want your life. Feed me, baby, feed me.

There are vampires and vampires, and the ones that suck blood are not the worst.

Count Dracula: Prince of Darkness

And last, but certainly not least, comes Dracula himself. Drawn from the ancient legends of Vlad Dracul's family, heavily embellished by the hand of Bram Stoker, we learn that the Count was a tall and visibly old man, clean-shaven except for a long white moustache (not something that is generally portrayed in movies), his body clad from head to foot in black without a single dash of colour on any part of his body.

Stoker enhances his hero's first impression by giving him the facility for perfect English but with a strange 'intonation' and great charm. His face, on closer examination, is strong, very strong and aquiline 'with high bridge of the thin nose and peculiarly arched nostrils; with lofty domed forehead, and hair growing scantily round the temples, but profusely elsewhere.'

The master's eyebrows were 'very massive', almost meeting across the top of his nose. His mouth, beneath the moustache, was peculiarly cruel-looking with disturbingly sharp white teeth which 'naturally' protruded over his lips, these in turn showing great vitality and redness for one so evidently old. His general complexion was one of pallor.

This combination of elegance and crudeness is brilliantly protrayed by Stoker's description of Dracula's hands –

Hitherto I had noticed the backs of his hands as they lay on his knees in the firelight, and they had seemed rather white and fine; but seeing them now close to me, I could not but notice that they were rather coarse broad, with squat fingers. Strange to say there were hairs in the centre of the palm. The nails were long and fine, and cut to a sharp point. As the Count leaned over to me and his hands touched me, I could not repress a shudder.

The master's breath, of course, smelled terrible, but then this would perhaps not have been so uncommon in days when cleanliness was not of the utmost importance. More significant may have been the fact that the close presence of Dracula simply caused Harker to almost faint.

Count Dracula has been rejuvenated a hundred times since Stoker wrote his famous novel, and there are many today who would dearly love to believe that the most monstrous of vampires still walks the silent and black hills of Romania, surviving all attempts to destroy him. Father of monsters, the most superb hypnotist, fabulous gentleman and the crudest of all killers. If he does, then the world is ultimately and forever a deadly place to be.

This combination of elegance and crudeness is brilliantly portrayed by Stoker's description of Dracula's hands.

is: sed destructâ essentiâ annihilatur ens; ergo sicuti à
ullâ vi creatâ anima potest annihilari, ita nec spoliari
ntrinsecâ activitate. Neque *b) in actu secundo.* Nam ut
is cogitandi et volendi ab omni actione impediri possit,
eberet vel *impedimentum aliquod poni,* vel *tolli omne ob-
ctum cogitabile vel appetibile:* atqui neutrum à vi creatâ
eri potest. *Non tolli omne objectum,* nam anima est sibi
psa objectum intimè praesens, potest itaque se suasque
utationes et affectiones percipere, et ex iis mediante
eâ τοῦ *esse simpliciter,* ratiocinando ad suam contingen-
am, atque hinc ad entis necessarii existentiam et varias
us perfectiones pervenire: ergo..... *Non poni impedimen-
m,* id enim deberet poni inter animam et objectum in
uod tendit: sed inter animam et animam, quae sibi ipsa
test esse objectum in quod tendat, nihil interponi post; ergo.....

O..........ES.

67. OBJ. 1. .... corpore non potest
istere. Nam anima ....dinatur ad efficien-
m cum corpore s.......... ...tam; ergo destructo
rpore, ex naturâ .... et ipsam perire.
R. N. **Assert.** A.......... Anima ex **naturâ suâ**
dinatur, id est, esse.......... ...inem habet ad effi-
ndam cum cor.......... ...pletam *hominis,*
Ant. Id est, e.......... ...necessariò semper
u esse conjunc.......... Non enim es..........

Chapter 6

The Vampire Library

The Horror House of Lords

In the library of any respectable vampire, there may be found many volumes that exemplify a long and rich history of literature surrounding the undead. We have already had a glimpse into the darker realms of Count Dracula, Lord Ruthven and other dangerous characters. Some of these have been given life and death only through human fantasy, while others actually lived and died in reality, such as the Countess Bathory.

The creation and continued spread of belief in vampire legends has been fuelled most effectively by its literature. If a vampire were to suffer an identity crisis, he or she would readily discover reassurance in the pages of books like *The Castle of Otranto* written by Horace Walpole in 1764. This book started a gothic revival, the authors of which professed to use all manner of methods, including drugs, heavy protein diets and even laughing gas, to bring about dreams of death and the dark arts to fuel their fiction.

One of the most famous groups to bring the dark side of the imagination to the surface was formed by Lord Byron, Mary and Percy Shelley, and Dr. Polidori, who reportedly spent many a candlelit evening in front of a large fire while staying in a villa near Lake Geneva. They created wonderful stories such as *Frankenstein*, by Mary Shelley and *The Vampyre* by Polodori in the early nineteenth century. The crude drug laudanum was employed to aid these bizarre imaginings and, once again, dreams were the fuel of fiction.

The writer of the most famous book of them all, the Irishman Bram Stoker, had written only one other volume before his classic study of Count Dracula. This was *Duties of Clerks of Petty Sessions in Ireland*, an unlikely work for the writer we associate today with the greatest vampire story in history. He suffered a terrible nightmare in 1890, while still working in Ireland as a business manager, and the bestselling *Dracula* changed his life forever. But this and other works of the same period were certainly not the first attempts to relate the oldest legends in mankind's history.

As we will see in more detail in the next chapter about the darkest origins of the vampire, the story began even with Adam himself, whose first wife Lilith sucked blood and ate small children, and whose dreadful daughters, the Lilim, pestered priests in their dreams and generally made unpleasant nuisances of themselves. Earliest man was accustomed to draining human blood in sacrifice to the gods and it was believed that Mother Earth would not allow a good harvest if the seasonal rituals were not conscientiously performed with the slaughter of some poor innocent on the land.

There is a difference between the early stories which gave rise to the medieval folklore of vampirism, described in earlier parts of this book, and the more modern gothic or romantic approach to the undead which appeared during the eighteenth and nineteenth centuries. It is the difference between the ghastly, blood-ravaging horror of true sacrifice and bloody slaughter, and a much sexier and more acceptable version which appeared later in fiction. In the original folkloric accounts, vampires, werewolves and other horrific legendary creatures would leap on the victim, smother their face with a hairy, foul-smelling rear end, and rip the chest open to gorge like a wild animal on the twitching corpse. There was nothing remotely romantic, engaging, intellectual, or even faintly human about such an attack, and the generally messy process probably took a matter of minutes before it was all over. This is certainly not the stuff of bestselling novels. Following the eighteenth century

In the original folkloric accounts, vampires, werewolves and other horrific legendary
creatures would leap on the victim, smother their face with a hairy, foul-smelling rear
end, and rip the chest open to gorge like a wild animal on the twitching corpse.

Max Schreck as the vampire Count Orlok in the film *Nosferatu*, shot in 1921 by German Expressionist director FW Murnau.

gothic revival, the vampire became a tall, gaunt, well-dressed figure with an extensive knowledge of worldly affairs gleaned from hundreds of years of travel and culture. He served fine wines and good food at his table (though partook of none himself), entertained his guests with intellectual repartee, and eventually seduced his female victims using a mesmeric stare, fine looks and promises of sexual bliss. The kill was transferred from the chest cavity to the neck with implications, barely hidden, of sexual penetration and eternal servitude. The unbeatable book *Interview with the Vampire,* written by Anne Rice, transformed the romantic version of the vampire still further and brought it soundly into the present day, with wonderful hints of passion, underworld secrets and the deepest, darkest realms of magic.

So from the rather disgusting vampire monsters created by writers such as Tournefort in the late seventeenth century, who fed from animals, drank huge amounts of alcohol, and stank of every unpleasant odour, we find ourselves more involved thereafter with clean-shaven, pale-faced seducers dressed in black tie and tails.

The aristocratic vampire rose to fame above his less desirable ancestors partly because of the most notorious of the nineteenth century lords, the poet

Byron himself. Byron flourished both on his reputation as a writer and as a ladykiller. In fact it was rumoured in the gossip columns of nineteenth century Paris and London that he had murdered his mistress and drank her blood from a cup made out of her skull.

The stories and gossip surrounding Byron were given additional strength by a series of literary and amorous events that would today happily grace the worst newspaper front covers. During a torrid and disastrous affair between Lord Byron and Lady Caroline Lamb, which ended in 1815, much acrimony flew between the two participants. Lady Caroline wrote a gothic novel entitled *Glenarvon* which quite obviously parodied her ex-lover in the most scurrilous manner in the character of Clarence de Ruthven, Lord Glenarvon. The book was published in the spring of 1816.

Later that same year Polidori wrote his version of Lord Byron's feverish activities in *Vampyre*, the main character of which was named simply 'Lord Ruthven', of whom we have heard much already. Polidori evidently lifted the character for Ruthven directly out of Lady Lamb's book. But that wasn't all in this tale of complex aristocratic intrigue. Polidori's book was left unpublished for three years, then picked up by the same publisher as Lady Lamb's book, who published it as though it had been written by Byron himself. Lord Ruthven became a kind of vampiric Batman, appearing in various forms by various well-known authors around Europe during the rest of the nineteenth century, until the idea of Byron as aristocratic vampire was almost established as a direct connection.

All this fantasy and intrigue among the nobility and leading socialites served to bring the erotic, aristocratic creature of darkness into our lives today.

Other vampires that we have met also graced the pages of this same romantic period of literature. James Malcolm's *Varney, the Vampire*, published in 1846, was known as a 'penny-dreadful' because of the cheap nature of its comic-like format. The story was published in serial form, comprising a massive 800 pages, and was subjected to much critical anxiety because of its graphic content, much of which had been lifted directly from Polidori's book *The Vampyre*. The series also borrowed one of its major scenes from Mary Shelley's story, *Frankenstein*, where the monster leaps into Mount Vesuvius.

One of the most obvious aspects of Count Dracula's character was his sexuality, for the dreaded aristocrat of the dark forest and gloomy night was one of the sexiest creatures ever to grace the pages of Gothic fiction.

The combination of Lord Byron, Mary Shelley and Polidori, sitting in their villa next to Lake Geneva, was responsible, it seems, for a great deal of the output that occurred in vampire literature later that century.

But James Malcolm Rymer's book about Varney the Vampire wasn't entirely unoriginal and formed part of the chain of creativity that eventually helped to give life to Count Dracula himself. Within the ghastly meanderings that the story takes, there appears a certain Hungarian count who is also a vampire and the first to appear in English vampiric literature. Sir Francis Varney, the aristocratic vampire of the story, was not exactly the Dracula-type but many of his characteristics found their way into Bram Stoker's masterpiece, mixed and matched, quite obviously, from one writer to another. One of the most important features of this chain of developing ideas was that a male vampire could hypnotize a female victim and then, through a mixture of sexual attraction and the exchange of blood, create a kind of tormenting love/hate relationship. We can see that this was yet another incarnation of the patriarchal social values that were so strong in the nineteenth century.

The Literary Dracula

Bram Stoker's sources for the writing of *Dracula* came from fact, fiction and his dreams. According to modern literary sleuths, Stoker drew his material from little-known works of travelogue, including *Untrodden Paths in Roumania*, which contains a wealth of information concerning the awesome Vlad Dracul the Impaler, and *Midst The Wild Carpathians*, which is a fictional work describing life in Hungary under the dark-light of devilish deeds. Count Azzo von Klatka, whom we met briefly earlier, perhaps provided some of the methods by which Dracula dealt with his unfortunate victims, and it is also said that Stoker took much from Wilkie Collins's classic novel *The Woman in White*. But Stoker's *Dracula* was in no way simply a derivative of other creations. At the time of his terrible dream in 1890, Stoker was the business manager of actor Henry Irving, one of the biggest stage names of the period. In his book *Vampyres*, Christopher Frayling suggests that the count's theatrical

Considered the most important author in his genre, Bram Stoker's sources for the writing of *Dracula* came from fact, fiction and his own dreams.

behaviour, the swirling cloaks and loud voice, may have been inspired by Henry Irving's real-life character. This dramatic characterization was just one small part of the jigsaw puzzle that resulted in the inimitable Count. Much of the rest was drawn, as we have seen, from the ghastly doings of the Hungarian Prince Vlad, a remote ancestor of Attila the Hun. But Count Dracula lived in Transylvania, not Hungary. He was a Count, not a Prince, and there could not have been the slightest chance that Dracula slaughtered his victims in quite so messy a fashion as did Vlad the Impaler.

This extraordinary combination of real and imagined horror, however, had another aspect to it, an aspect which may have been inspired by a further source. Stoker suffered from one of the most unpleasant diseases of his era, syphilis. Syphilis was in the nineteenth century what AIDS is today, or the bubonic plague was in the Middle Ages. There was no cure, and sufferers died an unpleasant death. Stoker, while living under the threat of death, experienced the only known human condition that truly resembles vampirism, that

The extraordinary universe created by Stoker in his novel was represented in the film *Dracula* by Francis Ford Coppola.

of congenital syphilis. A child born with syphilis suffers certain horrific dysfunctions which are similar to many of the most ancient descriptions of vampirism. It could well have occurred to Stoker that this was a genuine source for belief surrounding the undead.

The syphilitic child may be born with all its front teeth shaped like incisors (a condition known as Hutchinson's Teeth), sharply pointed, and ranged across the upper and lower gums exactly like those traditionally depicted in vampires. The eyes suffer from a condition which renders them pale and often encircled by a dark ring. The result is light blindness, in other words the sufferer can see only in the dark. The palate structure is deformed so that only liquids may be ingested, and the bridge of the nose collapses. Babies born with congenital syphilis would also cause the mother's breast skin to rot.

This appalling condition resembles vampirism to such an extent that it might well have formed the basis for vampiric legends over the centuries. We can at least state with certainty that Bram Stoker would have been entirely familiar with this horrific condition.

In contrast to all this gory unpleasantness, the other notable aspect of Count Dracula's character was his sexuality, for the dreaded aristocrat of the dark forest and gloomy night was one of the sexiest creatures ever to grace the pages of gothic fiction. In probably the strangest collection of contrasts any reader could hope to find, Bram Stoker created Dracula as a hybrid, part animal, part blue-blooded Lord, part serial killer, part genetic aberration, part immortal, and a very large part hypnotically powerful lover. Almost as though Stoker was concocting the ultimate dream of the dark side, perhaps inspired by the very deepest realms of his own strange life, the jigsaw puzzle of Dracula's character is brought to its final piquancy by the clear inference of sexual dominance over his unfortunate (though perhaps Stoker felt they were fortunate) victims.

Each woman that Dracula made love to, including Lucy Westenra, became immortal, stunningly beautiful, everlastingly young and far more attractive than ever they were before the dread vampire had performed his dastardly deed. Here again, as in everything Victorian, Stoker makes no direct mention of the vampire having sexual intercourse with his victims, but the descriptions that depict the sucking of blood through deep penetration of the incisors, speak volumes of other more gentle activities happening concurrently.

Polidori's Vampyre

Perhaps still more significant in some ways than Stoker's *Dracula*, was Dr. John Polidori's *Vampyre*, concerning ostensibly the terrible activities of one Lord Ruthven.

Polidori was born to an Italian immigrant family living in Central London's Soho neighbourhood. His father was a literary translator of some considerable talent and fame, and son John made it early to university to study medicine. In fact, he was one of the youngest graduating students in England at the time, passing his examinations in 1815 at the tender age of 19. Shortly after leaving Edinburgh University he became Lord Byron's physician and suffered a tumultuous half year at the hands of the temperamental poet aristocrat, leaving his service in the summer of 1816, and thereafter returning to London to write up his experiences as a fiction in the form of the life of Lord Ruthven. The story is clearly a description of the time he spent with Byron, with added 'juice' and considerable anger, for Byron was apparently not a happy man to work with. Polidori did not seek publication of his short work and began a novel entitled *Emestus Berchtold* which disappeared without trace. By 1820 he was clearly suffering from the effects of severe brain damage, and in August 1821 he died at the age of 25. It was believed by some that he committed suicide using prussic acid, though there is some evidence that this was not the case.

The final years of his tragic, short life were not enhanced by the actions of Lord Byron's publishers and, subsequently, Paris literary society. The short story *Vampyre* was published in 1819 under Byron's name (though Byron did not know he was supposed to have written it, even after publication). The story soon became a massive hit in Paris.

Literary critics attributed the work to Lord Byron and insisted no one else could possibly have written it, ignoring Polidori completely. The short story caught the public's imagination and inspired other works of art, including a full-length novel entitled *Lord Ruthven ou Les Vampires*, which was dedicated to Lord Byron and written as a sort of nineteenth-century 'novel-after-the-movie'. At the same time, no less than three plays hit the stages of the capital and ran concurrently: *Le Vampire* staged at the Porte-Saint-Martin theatre, *Le Vampire* staged at the Vaudeville theatre, and *Les Trois Vampires* at the Variétés theatre, all based on the story of Ruthven's life.

All this, happening behind poor Polidori's back, might easily have been enough to drive him to prussic acid and an early ignoble death. His fee for writing the original story, eventually paid in retrospect by the fraudulent publishers of the work, was about 50 dollars. Such acts of violation today would surely result in multimillion dollar law suits.

Polidori's work was perhaps the single most significant contribution to the aristocratic, sexy, monstrous vampire cult that continued throughout the rest of the nineteenth century and still stands as a basis for romantic Gothic-horror fiction today. Even the work of Anne Rice and Stephen King, and other contemporary horror-fiction writers, must attribute a great deal to the unfortunate Dr. Polidori. And yet, the dreaded spectre of death conjured up by the writers of the nineteenth century bears little or no relation to the 'real' vampire. In fact, if we take a look at the earliest derivations of the word 'vampire' itself, we find that its common roots in most Mediterranean languages come from 'vam' meaning blood and 'pyr' meaning monster, and this blood-monster was in no way aristocratic, sexy, cultured, suave or immortal, just simply very, very nasty.

Chapter 7

Awesome Beginnings

We saw in the last chapter how mankind has imagined his favourite vampire in recent centuries. The enduring image of the powerful, elegant and yet animal–like vampire is very much alive, but its most distant ancestors are a very different story.

In all the darkest pages of the malign supernatural there is no more terrible tradition than that of the Vampire, a pariah even among demons. Foul are his ravages; gruesome and seemingly barbaric are the ancient and approved methods by which folk must rid themselves of this hideous pest. Even today in certain quarters of the world, in remoter districts of Europe itself, Transylvania, Slavonia, the isles and mountains of Greece, the peasant will take the law into his own hands and utterly destroy the carrion who – as it is yet firmly believed – at night will issue from his unhallowed grave to spread the infection of vampirism throughout the countryside. Assyria knew the vampire long ago, and he lurked amid the primeval forests of Mexico before Cortes came. He is feared by the Chinese, by the Indian and the Malay alike; whilst Arabian story tells us again and again of the ghouls who haunt ill-omened sepulchres and lonely cross-ways to attack and devour the unhappy traveller.

This introductory paragraph begins the 1928 book written by Montague Summers entitled *The Vampire – His Kith and Kin* (published in London by Kegan Paul, Trech, Trubner and Co.) with a perfect summary of the awesome origins of the undead. So be prepared to enter now the very darkest realm of all, the most slippery, slimy, blood-ridden cul-de-sac in all of mankind's legendary corridors.

Corridors of Glower

Much of the early discussion surrounding the vampire myth was related to attempts to define exactly what they were. Definition was a matter of great importance, both in medieval Europe and during the early part of the twentieth century when Montague Summers's book was written. Both these periods were concerned with reason as a method of discounting the irrationality of the devil. In other words, if you could define something then perhaps you could control it.

The first question raised was, is a vampire a fallen angel? The answer came back quickly that it was not, even though fallen angels could count among their number the intrepid 'Nick', devil incarnate, because angels were not corporeal. By contrast, vampires had solid bodies. Thus, angels were acquitted at least of this dread fate.

So perhaps the vampire is simply a demon in disguise. In order to decide whether this potential inhuman cap fits the much-despised undead, we need to ask what characteristics a demon exhibits? Demons are known to enter living bodies and take possession of them, but demons do not have bodies of their own. They are, so to speak, the worst kind of squatters. But we could say this also of the vampire, for vampiric possession takes place, or so we have been led to believe, once the departing spirit of the dead has returned and taken up residence again, either in its own body or that of some other poor person. But there is a difference. The demon can pop in and out, while the vampire is stuck inside the body it occupies. So, all ye demons may rest assured that this fate is not thine. Though it does need to be pointed out that demons and vampires

The first question was, is a vampire a fallen angel?

have a lot in common and could no doubt be discovered on a cold dark night sniggering together on foggy country lanes, presumably comparing notes on matters of lust and horridness.

Then how about ghosts and phantoms? Is there any chance that these share the same dusty coffin as the vampire? Once again the answer is no, and for the same reason, that a ghost ain't got no body. The fact is, the vampire has a body, and it is his own body. He may even be proud of it, as was (is) Lord Ruthven. But that body is neither alive nor dead. Instead, it lives in death, almost as though the vampire has crossed over to the other side and taken a human body with it.

Having come to this conclusion, the early writers and students of mythology moved along to the next step in their sometimes tortured reckonings as to the accountability of the undead state. If death was considered by the living to be a place of rest, and it was established that vampires continued to live in death, then the fate of the vampire was perhaps not unpleasant. However, particularly in theological circles of debate, the power of reason was thickly clouded with dogma and thus tended to come out both overheated and fuzzy. People were supposed to accept that an immortal life was undesirable because the Church said so, regardless of what might really be the case. Excessive interest in sex was also considered to be bad news for the same reason, and the ability of the vampire to overpower and generally dominate normal living humans was definitely not a good thing, even though the medieval Church was torturing and terrifying everyone in sight throughout Europe. It was okay for God to do this, but no one else could.

Vampires, therefore, exactly mirrored the worst fears of the pious and perfect. Vampires were dangerous, sexually rampant, enormously powerful, absolutely unconcerned about human dignity and preservation of the soul, and finally... dead. And it was this last aspect of their nature that made them the most fascinating to legend-makers. They had overcome the one great stigma of life: that dark place which could never be explained nor controlled. And therefore there was only one possible conclusion: they had to be grossly unhappy about it. It was not until the gothic romantics of Byron's era that a few of the more imaginative writers decided that perhaps vampirism could be a desirable state. But even then, because of the Church's continued force, the pleasure of immortal sexual passion had ultimately to be destroyed by a stake in the heart. You could not afford to allow someone like Lord Ruthven to survive. He might eventually persuade too many people that being a vampire was just fine. So if we delve back into the darkest shadows of vampiric history we find ourselves faced with just one phenomenon with which to begin: death.

Death Lies Bleeding

Given that man expresses his fear of wrongdoing through guilt, we can understand that primitive man might have understood his ability to kill through a fear that anything which he deprived of life might well come back to haunt him. If I slaughter an animal, I might be afraid that the animal will, in some way, take revenge upon me. I value life so much, after all. Worse, if I kill a human being, that departing soul will very likely take its revenge upon me by sucking my blood, the life-force of my existence.

So we might easily find the source of the vampire at the very outset of mankind's attempted comprehension of life and death. Primitive man would have observed his friends and family standing and moving around in life. He would then have observed the fact that the same people suddenly laid down and ceased to move. The body became static. But how could life suddenly stop? Surely something else simply replaced the body and continued to live in a place that was not visible? Thus the soul was born invisible, elsewhere after life, and holy. Because life was bad and difficult, by contrast, what happened after life must be good and relatively easy and enjoyable.

But, by contrast, anything that could go to heaven must on the other hand have the choice to go to hell, and in hell lay all the things that mankind considered unworthy, his fantasies and the forbidden fruits he dared not think about. And here lay the seed of the vampire, buried in unhallowed earth among the dirt of unknown death.

Ritual magic and religion were closely linked, with the devil being behind all evil and all dark mischief. His presence was a kind of reassurance that limits existed, beyond which humanity could not step.

Ancient tribes worshipped their dead as much as they did their gods. Kings, especially, were worshipped after death. But then mankind has still not lost that propensity, for kings, presidents and even prime ministers are worshipped through the study of history, and the erection of statues today. We still maintain a reverence for the dead, may they rest in peace. And this is why the vampire myth has never died, for we feel respect for what happens after life, perhaps even more than we respect what happens in life.

And how many gods have required blood to be sacrificed to them? In order that the earth should continue to provide rich harvests, the blood of mankind should be spread across the ground. Mother Earth the vampire.

African tribes such as the Ovambo, who occupy the Bantu areas of South West Africa, will cut off the head and limbs of the dead in order to curtail the return of too many spirits into the world of the living. Their belief is that a careful spirit population control must be practiced or trouble will follow. This may have been one of the earliest religious ideas to find its way into modern vampiric legend. One of the few foolproof methods of finishing off a vampire is to cut off its head and limbs. This way the spirit cannot 'walk abroad' and cause trouble anymore.

The Caffre tribe believes that the dead may return and become rejuvenated by human blood, coming back from death specifically to drink the human liquid. Members of the tribe are horrified by dropped blood and will cover it on the ground, even if it falls from a bleeding nose or cut hand. An evil spirit might, after all, take up the single drop of blood and reincarnate as something hideously evil. Blood for almost all of the world's cultures has formed the very foundation for superstition and magic.

For the life of the flesh is in the blood: therefore I said unto the children of Israel: You shall not eat the blood of any flesh at all, because the life of the flesh is in the blood, and whosoever eateth it, shall be cut off.

Even animals had to be drained of their blood before being eaten, and only the worst black magic cult practices would make use of the blood of creatures for their dark worship.

Aboriginal tribes in Australia acknowledge the life-giving nature of blood for the living.

But as with everything, there is always an opposite. Aboriginal tribes in Australia acknowledge the life-giving nature of blood for the living and make very little discrimination for the dead, believing that death is merely a step along the way. As part of their death rituals they will scratch the body of the deceased soon after death so that blood spills onto the ground. The idea is that the blood will give the deceased's soul a helping hand along the way to the next part of the trip. This most ancient of rituals would fit neatly into the concept that the dead need blood from the living.

Naming the Dead

At the end of the last chapter we made brief reference to the origin of the word 'vampire'. In many of the Mediterranean tongues the root, as we saw, came from words meaning 'blood-monster'. In other languages, such as those closer to Dracula's home, there are similar meanings. The very earliest reference to the word arises in Slavonia in the Magyar form *vampir*, which is the same in Russian, Polish, Czech, Serbian and Bulgarian, with some variations: *vapir, vepir, veryr, vopyr, upier*. In Lithuanian derivations there is an interesting variation on the idea of the vampire being not just a blood-monster but a blood-drunk. The word that gives rise to the idea of a vampire is a mixture of *wempti*, meaning to drink, and *wampiti*, to growl or mutter. So the use of that word gives an intonation of drunkenness. In Croatia the word for a vampire was *pijauica*, meaning one who is red-faced with drink. In Albania the name for vampire means the restless dead, and in Greece and the surrounding territories there is no word for vampire at all. In European languages, the name has always been somewhat similar: Danish and Swedish use *vampyr*, Dutch uses *vampir*, in French it is *vampire*, Italian, Spanish and Portuguese use *vampiro*, and modern Latin *vampyrus*. In early editions of the *Oxford English Dictionary*, the definition is:

> *A preternatural being of a malignant nature (in the original unusual form of the belief an animated Corpse), supposed to seek nourishment and do harm by sucking the blood of sleeping persons; a man or woman abnormally endowed with similar habits.*

Ascending the Vampire Line

We use the term Dark Ages to describe a period of history quite simply because that's what they were. The records and structure of civilization put in place by the Romans were destroyed at the end of the Empire and for 400 years Europe seems to have been plunged into darkness and chaos.

Many of the ancient traditions that had been around since Babylonian and Assyrian times were reinstated during these years, as magic became darker, witches became more powerful and monsters were seen on every corner. There were even carefully considered prescriptions for conditions under which the dead would rise again.

> *Whether thou art a ghost unburied,*
> *Or a ghost that none careth for,*
> *Or a ghost with none to make offerings to it,*
> *Or a ghost that hath none to pour libations to it,*
> *Or a ghost that hath no prosperity.*

Or–

> He that lieth in a ditch,
> He that no grave covereth,
> He that lieth uncovered,
> Whose head is uncovered with dust,
> The king's son that lieth in the desert,
> Or in the ruins. The hero whom they have slain with the sword.

Or–

> He that hath died of hunger in prison,
> He that hath died of thirst in prison,
> The hungry man who in his hunger hath not smelt the smell of food,
> He whom the bank of a river hath made to perish,
> He that hath died in the desert or marshes,
> He that a storm hath overwhelmed in the desert,
> The Night-wraith that hath no husband,
> The Night-fiend that hath no wife,
> He that hath posterity and he that hath none.

It was tough not to be a vampire in those days!

The line of ascendency of the vampire is, in broad terms, easy to trace. If ever there was one vampire that has lived the whole span of tradition, he would be more or less 3,000 years old today. The peoples of the Assyrian and Babylonian empires were, as far as have been documented, the first to deal with difficult spirits and walking dead.

The myth and tradition of the Ekimmu, the persistent haunter believed to exist by ancient civilizations, survived into the Dark Ages and through into modern times in eastern Europe, where it is still said to be found today in countries such as Romania and Transylvania. Monsters that range through the night, raping, sucking blood and murdering, have now even found their way into American culture, where vampires have hardly been documented at all in the past. The modern vampire is the serial killer who entices innocent people into his home, defiles them in one way or another, murders them, then eats the body. Vampirism has truly hardly changed in over 3,000 years. The only real difference has been the ways in which various cultures through history have dealt with the vampire and his friends.

In ancient Assyria, incantations were used against any evil spirit that reincarnated and took advantage of human flesh. The Ekimmu would be driven from the underworld by hunger and thirst, and when no offerings or sacrifices were made at the tomb, so the monster would partake of human flesh and blood instead. The same belief structure also existed in ancient Chinese mythology, particularly among Buddhists. And it is here that we find one of the origins of the idea that vampires can survive only at night. His wanderings were believed to begin when the sun went to rest, and to end when the first rays of morning drove him back into his grave. The very beginning of this superstition was, of course, the god of the sun himself, who had power over all of earth's activities. His powers even stretched to stopping home fires, making umbrellas potentially unlucky, and many other now forgotten capabilities. (The old superstition related to opening an umbrella indoors was because the umbrella was originally only used by priests as protection against too much sun. It was known as a sun-wheel. To open an umbrella indoors was to insult the dominion of the sun.)

But above all other fears that have existed throughout the ascendency of the undead, the one most frightening was that associated with the epidemic nature of vampiric attack. If the vampire sucked enough blood from his victim, so that victim became a vampire too.

The bubonic plague, known as 'the pestilence' or 'the black death', ravaged Europe from the Far East during several dark periods of medieval history. It was the population leveller. It appeared in parts of the countryside like a dark, noxious wind, slaughtered thousands of hapless people in a matter of weeks and then melted away again. It was the greatest fear of the ages, and no one seemed able to do anything about it. In the fourteenth century it is said to have killed around one-third of the world's population, and people at the time believed that it would wipe out mankind altogether before it left. With such deeply rooted experience, the idea of pestilence and epidemic was strong in the medieval mind, and the creation of the vampiric legend was at least partly insired by these deep-seated fears. It is interesting to note that many of the original characteristics of traditional vampiric myth seem to have come from China (as well as Assyria), and coincidentally so also did the first bubonic plague.

Far-Far East

In the Indian folktale *Vikram and the Vampire*, the monster is called the *Baital-Pachisi* and arises from an ancient Hindu tradition. In the story, the hero Raja encounters the creature hanging upside-down in a very Indian style, from the branch of a tree. It was

> *head downwards from a branch, a little above him. Its eyes, which were wide open, were of greenish-brown, and never twinkled; its hair also was brown and brown was its face, these several shades which, notwithstanding, approached one another in an unpleasant way, as in an over-dried coconut. Its body was thin and ribbed like a skeleton or a bamboo framework, and as it held on to a bough, like a flying-fox, by the tips of its toes, its drawn muscles stood out as if they were ropes of coir. Blood it appeared to have none, or there would have been a decided determination of that curious juice to the head; and as Raja handled its skin, it felt icy cold and clammy as might a snake. The only sign of life was the whisking of a ragged little tail much resembling a goat's. Judging from these signs the brave king at once determined the creature to be a Baital, a Vampire.*

By contrast in Malaysia, vampires were believed to look more like gigantic mosquitoes, not surprisingly. The *Penanggalan* was a trunkless human head with a stomach hanging from the neck, which flew about sucking the blood of hapless victims, particularly children. By its description it might seem that it was specifically created to frighten children into behaving themselves and had no other role than this.

Among the endlessly imaginative myths of the Far East there is another which brings us a kind of female vampire called the *Langsuior* who originally

"The vampire lurked amid the primeval forests of Mexico before Cortes came."

arose from a very beautiful woman who gave birth to a stillborn child. She was so distressed that she transformed into a vampiric form, flew from where she stood and remained for the rest of her life perched in trees. She always wore a green robe and had tapering nails of extraordinary length (a mark of beauty in Malaysia), like talons. Her hair was long and jet black, almost to her ankles, and concealed a hole in the back of her neck through which she sucked the blood of children.

In the description from which we have learned of this vampirish female there is something of a give-away as to the original source. The method advised by the writer for dealing with the *Langsuior* entails cutting off most of her hair, stuffing the long tresses into the hole in the back of her neck, and cutting off her long fingernails. The description of this method is completed with the following phrase:

> *...in which case she will become quiet and domesticated, just like an ordinary woman...!*

It may be that the hole in the back of her neck was simply switched from the front, and her fingernails, to be cut to the quick, were really a metaphor for taming an undomesticated woman so she gives up her habit of making the writer's life difficult.

From this male chauvinist source came the female vampire, and the later European version of the same superstition brought the story forward in a similar format:

> *If a woman dies in childbirth, either before delivery or after the birth of the child, and before the 40 days of uncleanness have expired, she is popularly supposed to become a 'langsuyar', a flying demon of the nature of the white lady or banshee. To prevent this, a quantity of glass beads are put in the mouth of the corpse, a hen's egg is put under each armpit, and needles are placed in the palms of the hands. It is believed that if this is done, the dead woman cannot become a 'langsuyar' as she cannot open her mouth to shriek or wave her arms as wings or open and shut her hands to assist the flight.*

In the Indian folktale *Vikram and the Vampire*, the monster is called the *Baital-Pachisi* and arises from an ancient Hindu tradition.

In Polynesia we find the *tu* or *talamaur* which eats chunks from his victims and then somehow becomes their friend or familiar. His favourite habit is to eat the flesh of a freshly dead person and thus absorb the final vitality from the body. But finally, perhaps the most convincing source for the dark seat of the vampire legend, is the West Indies, where vampirism was brought from what was earlier in the twentieth century known as Guinea and the Congo, and maintained by African slaves.

In Granada the vampire is called the *Loogaroo* and this unpleasant creature seems to have been born out of a hybrid of the early French colonists' superstitions and the African voodoo that it came to destroy.

Loogaroos are human, especially females, who have made a pact with the devil by which they are given magical powers on condition that they provide their master with fresh warm blood each night. Each night, the *loogaroo* visits the *bombax ceiba* tree, an occult silk-cotton tree, also known in the region as the Devil's tree or the Jumbie tree. Once there, the *loogaroo* slips out of its skin, carefully folds it up and hides it under the tree or a nearby bush and then speeds about the local area to fulfil its task. Once the skin is taken off, the *loogaroo* becomes concealed by turning its skinless body into a ball of sulphurous fire. Anyone visiting Granada even today will be shown, on demand, the darting fire of the *loogaroo*.

The only way to protect the home against the vampire is to spread rice and sand about the entrance. The *loogaroo* cannot enter the house until it has counted every grain, and will therefore be there until morning, when the sunlight will send it screaming back to the Devil's tree for its skin.

Chapter 8

How to Kill a Vampire

ow does one kill fear, I wonder? How do you shoot a spectre through the heart, slash off its spectral head, take it by its spectral throat? It is an enterprise you rush into while you dream, and are glad to make your escape with wet hair and every limb shaking. The bullet is not run, the blade not forged, the man not born; even the winged words of truth drop at your feet like lumps of lead. You require for such a desperate encounter an enchanted and poised shaft dipped in a lie too subtle to be found on earth. An enterprise for a dream, my masters!

How, indeed, do we kill our vampire once found, for we are still not sure whether it be a vision, a dream, a nightmare or a glimpse into a reality 'too subtle to be found on earth...'

Over the centuries, villagers have devised a number of methods designed to prevent corpses from becoming vampires, some of which we have seen already. They are numerous and often contradictory in nature, varying from region to region. They have been tested countless times, however, and for all the deaths that may have been caused by the monster, other mortals have been spared to observe and pass on these techniques.

When all else fails, then one must kill, and here we describe the methods which have been proven to work, eradicating the evil so that no more lives can be taken. Both in prevention and in direct action, there is a series of steps that must be faithfully observed. Remember we are dealing with the forces of the supernatural and must therefore symbolically pass the boundaries of human experience and imbue ourselves with magical properties so that we may succeed in our goal. If vampires are creatures who inhabit an in-between world, as we have seen they are, then we must strike out in the same realm. Yet 'the bullet is not run, the blade not forged, the man not born.' However, vampires have been killed or, perhaps more accurately, given peace, since it is generally believed that the soul of a vampire is in a delirium, suffering, unable to extricate itself from the earthly, mortal ties which bind our own existence here. If the curse of vampirism is loathsome and tortuous to the vampire itself, what better service could one render to the creature than the liberation of its soul?

Preventing the Dead

The methods used for turning evil away and of preventing corpses from becoming vampires are many and diverse. Among them we may find mutilation of the corpse, physical restraint, curious funeral rites, and even deceptions intended to trick the spirit world.

One of the most widely used practices, which can be traced back to the antiquity of early man, is that of placing objects in the grave. These are believed to play the role of satisfying the corpse, of rendering it incapable of returning, and of satisfying or scaring away any evil force which may wish or be intent on interfering with it.

The dead were thought to rise and attack passers-by.
Bodies were carefully wrapped to prevent this.

bucket of water

bowl of food

spike

Coins were put inside the mouths of corpses in ancient Greece. With this gift, the dead person could pay Charon the boatman for his passage across the River Styx, so that the soul could rest in peace after death.

In many regions of the world food is provided for the dead, because it is generally believed that the other world is similar to ours and that they will need to eat. The belief is that food in the grave will prevent the corpse from feeding on the living. Foodstuffs may be solid or liquid, drinks are kept in jars and grains in bowls. Curiously, poppy seeds have often been found in burial grounds, possibly included for their apparent narcotic effects which would encourage the dead to sleep rather than walk about in the land of the living.

In order to prevent potential vampires from finding their way out of the grave, in some regions where they were feared, the deceased were often buried face down to prevent them seeing their way out of the coffin.

If the dead needed food, the ancient mind reasoned they were also in need of work. In many agricultural villages a sickle, the archetypal symbol of reaping the harvest, was buried in the grave with a body. This is possibly the origin of the portrayal of death as a skeleton carrying a sickle, the grim reaper who takes lives.

Both food and work implements were intended to keep the corpse busy and satisfied so that there was no desire to return to the world of the living. These practices thus presupposed that all dead people had a real desire to come back and be part of life again, and that unless specific measures were taken to prevent this from happening they would certainly return.

Romania invented an automatic vampire-piercing device which consisted of one or several sharpened stakes, similar to those used by Prince Dracula for his impalements, driven into the grave so that when the body tried to rise out of it, it would be automatically pierced and killed without the villagers having to be on constant alert for a vampire insurgence.

In many instances skeletons have been found lying in their graves with their knees and/or wrists tied, and others, generally found in Bulgaria, have been rolled up inside carpets. These were clearly means of deterring *with force* the corpse from getting up and claiming victims from the nearby villages. The ropes that tied the limbs were hardly ever knotted since it was believed that the presence of knots in a grave would prevent the dead person from making an easy transition to the afterlife. Variations on funeral rites are a constant source of wonder. In one region of Romania, in Vrancea, it is said that it is unwise to cry over the dead. Instead, the family and friends must dance and sing so that any evil spirits in the vicinity will imagine they are observing a festivity, not a burial. Sometimes, two men who are especially strong will take hold of the deceased and dance with him in the hope that any observing spirits will believe that he is not dead at all.

On the other hand, in southern Italy, Spain and Greece, and in many other Catholic countries, it is ill-advised not to cry when someone dies. Paid mourners are engaged to wail noisily behind the funeral procession so that the deceased feels he or she has been properly loved and missed and is thus not tempted to come back.

In antiquity in such diverse regions as western Europe, Latin America and ancient Egypt, death was considered a slow process of transition from one state (life) to another (death). In such societies the burial, which occured soon after death, was temporary and provisional. The funeral marked the start of a long period during which a person was neither fully alive nor fully dead. During this period the corpse decomposed and the flesh decayed until only the bones remained. Next came the rites of secondary burial, during which the bones of the deceased were uncovered, ritually treated, and moved to a new location where they would permanently rest.

It was the sites of first burial that struck most fear into the minds of the villagers and they were therefore usually set further away from the perimeter of the village than the secondary burial ground, to ensure that the spirits failed to find their way back home. It was believed that in the first instance, the dead were seeking to make the passage from this to the afterworld, and this was therefore the most vulnerable period since anything could disturb their transition and compel them to return to the land of the living.

In many cultures of the world, including our own, the buried body is weighed down with blocks of stone. Tombstones, decorated with angels of peace, are a last remnant of this tradition, and the angel is intended to bring peace to the soul and help it through its passage from death to the afterlife.

In southern Italy, Spain and Greece, and in many other Catholic countries around the world, it is ill-advised not to cry in the cemetery.

Many perfectly natural phenomena led people to believe that in the first burial grounds, the dead were not really dead at all. One good example is *ignis fatuus*, or will-o'-the-wisp, seen so often at night burning over fresh graves. The 'little fire' was thought to be the flame of the soul still burning even after death, in much the same way as fairies appeared to humans in a transparent cloud or as little flames dancing over flowers at night. These two phenomena were taken for granted, and still are, and were considered to be supernatural visitations from a world, unknown to us, whose existence was parallel to ours. Now we know that a decomposing body produces great quantities of methane, a highly flammable gas, which mixes with other flammable gases when rising up through the ground, then mixes with oxygen, which in turn ignites the methane.

The shifting of fresh graves was another, quite natural, phenomenon which convinced people that the dead were really not fully dead. There is a period of time during which the earth in a grave undergoes a certain amount of readjusting and settling, and cracks may appear on its rocky surface. This was taken as sure sign that the dead were trying to escape from the burial site.

The secondary burial, on the other hand, was believed to be a place of peace since the dead had successfully completed their transition and were now not only at rest, but safely away from the human realm. Exhumations were carried out at the first burial plots, the remains were burned, and the ashes placed within urns. This process is very similar to the Catholic method of dealing with the remains of the dead used in southern Europe today.

In many modern cemeteries there is an organized way of moving around the remains as more space becomes available. Exhumations are a matter of course and, after a suitable period, which may vary from seven to 20 years, the bones are taken out of the grave, burned, and the remains placed elsewhere. Is this practice simply due to practical reasons, or is it based on the rituals that have been undertaken without interruption since ancient Celtic times?

Many cemeteries in Italy also employ the practical habit of exhuming bodies after a period of time, breaking the remaining bones so that the body takes up less space and then burying them again in smaller coffins to save space. This, too, is no doubt related to ancient practices.

It was during these exhumations that vampires were discovered. The natural expectation would have been to find a skeleton. We can imagine the surprise that an undecomposed body would have afforded cemetery caretakers. In order to prevent this from happening, many cultures opted for a different way to deal with dead bodies, the more reliable method of cremation. The bodies were cremated immediately after death and before burial to prevent the corpse from becoming a revenant and returning to life.

However, cultures who cremate their dead are not those that have been afflicted by vampire epidemics in the past. But the matter is not quite that simple, since the energy requirements for cremation are high: an average 'adult body weighing 160 lb (73 kg), cremated in a purpose-built furnace fired by gas, and with the re-circulation of hot gases, is destroyed to ash in three-quarters to one hour of steady burning at a temperature around 1,600°F (870°C).' The total destruction of a body was thus, in antiquity, almost impossible. Often wooden pyres were used, as they are today throughout the Indian subcontinent, and were coated with oil to provide a better combustion for the body. The problem is not how big the fire is, but rather its ability to convey enough heat and for long enough to burn a body to ashes. In many countries, however, and especially in those villages affected by vampire epidemics, cremation was impractical and the villagers were thus forced by circumstances to bury the dead instead, thus risking their return.

Preventing the Vampire

Jf, despite the measures taken to prevent the dead becoming vampires, they are nevertheless born, then there are steps to prevent being attacked by them. Various substances are deemed effective. Among these garlic, the vampire chaser *par excellence*, is the most widely used. Vampires loathe garlic and its smell is so detestable that they never come near a house protected by it. Garlic used to be put into graves as a preventative measure, and was also hung round the necks of the family of the deceased, hung around rooms, especially around windows, doors and on bedheads. It was also rubbed onto door and window frames and even on farm animals to prevent an attack.

The use of garlic was adopted to cordon off epidemics. Both in the plague years and during vampire insurgences people added garlic to their diets and wore necklaces made from it. The highly commendable properties of garlic form a natural antibiotic and its use in food makes for a healthy diet.

Another useful device to keep potential vampires from sucking blood from the living was to insert a thorn under the tongue. No vampire likes to be pierced by his victim, though it is unlikely that, considering the vampire's enormous strength and hypnotic powers, the victim would get much of a chance to use the thorn during an attack.

As we have seen, there are many similarities between the plague and a vampire epidemic, for the latter was believed to be catching, like a nasty disease. The bad smell, the smell of death associated with the plague, was believed to be the cause of the illness since its true origin had not yet been discovered. In order to safeguard themselves from it, people used strong-smelling substances in the belief that these were a good antidote to bad smells. Garlic was one of these, except that its health-enhancing properties were the true medicine. Wolfsbane was another herb widely used, and this was used in the same way or in conjunction with garlic. Silver knives were placed under mattresses and cribs to further strengthen the anti-vampire barrier.

Feature films on vampires have spread the belief that the creatures fear the crucifix. However, there is scarcely any evidence that this is so, either in folklore or in fiction. The Church and God have, unfortunately, little to do with vampirism, excepting perhaps that some prayers might help the dead from returning, and suitable incantations are recited at funerals to help the soul find peace. However, prevention is all very well but there is no more effective method to deal with vampires than killing.

Killing the Vampire

The classic, well-tested method of killing a vampire is to drive a stake through its heart. The dramatic possibilities of this situation have always been irresistible to writers and film directors. The vampire is portrayed lying in its coffin, dressed beautifully in a tuxedo. The courageous vampire killer drives a stake through its heart, and then pounds on it with a mallet. The vampire's features are contorted by pain and the eyes transfixed in a hateful state. The creature screams, and suddenly hundreds of years appear in its face until it crumbles to dust or becomes a mummified corpse. The process of staking is not as simple as it might appear in horror movies. An old piece of fencing or whittled chair leg will not do. In Russia and throughout the Baltics, for example, the best wood for the purpose is ash, due to its magical properties. In Silesia, on the other hand, such stakes were carved from oakwood, and in Serbia from hawthorn, because vampires are highly allergic to thorns.

A vampire who has only been half-killed because the killer has run away in panic is a
thousand times more dangerous than an ordinary vampire.

In the absence of a stake, vampires have been known to be killed with a
silver dagger, although the operation proves more difficult, and the majority
of stories concerning a silver dagger are more likely to be associated with the
killing of werewolves, a subject needing another complete volume to examine. A stake driven with force into the centre of the heart is by far the best

The vampire's features are contorted by pain and
the eyes transfixed in a hateful stare. The creature
screams, and suddenly hundreds of years appear in
its face until it crumbles to dust or becomes a
mummified corpse. Here, Barbara Shelley is to
suffer this transformation in *Dracula, Prince of
Darkness,* by Terence Fisher (1966).

A number of additional steps can be taken after staking the dread creature. The heart can be cut out and burned, and its ashes scattered in the waters of a flowing river.

and most successful method. The bloating of decomposing bodies in the grave, once seen as proof of vampire activity, was believed to be an attempt of the soul, or whatever had taken possession of the body, to escape. The hole made with the stake would have provided a good way out. Certainly vampire killers could clearly see that something was escaping when they pierced a decomposing body.

In some accounts of vampire killings, we learn that after the piercing of the body had taken place, blood gushed high into the air. This can easily be explained by the pressure in the body built up by all the gases produced naturally during decomposition. The famous vampire groan which occurs

after the stake has pierced the heart is due to the lungs being compressed by the attack. Air and gases would be forced rather explosively through the trachea, producing, quite understandably, a shriek not unlike a cry of terror from a living person. It may be, however, that a vampire genuinely groans as its soul attains its much longed-for liberation. There is invariably both a clear scientific, as well as a good irrational, explanation and no reason to suppose that either one is false... or true.

A number of additional steps can be taken after staking the dread creature. The heart can be cut out and burned, and its ashes scattered in the waters of a flowing river. In 1874 a Romanian prince settled in Paris after being forced into exile because members of his family were believed by their compatriots to turn into vampires on their deaths. The young prince cut out his own heart while he was dying to prevent himself from turning into a vampire. These were desperate measures indeed.

Some people cover the vampire with a shroud or a piece of cloth before staking it, in case the blood spills over them and transforms them into vampires too. For the super-neurotic, all or several of these remedies may be undertaken together, often resulting in a terrible and gory mess. So we find that sometimes not only is the heart cut out and burned, and thrown into water, but the head is chopped off, the corpse reburied at a crossroads, and the coffin filled with poppy seeds and other magic charms. Every possibility is covered to make really sure that the vampire is killed.

In the case of a vampire plague in France, the Pope was forced to conse-crate the River Rhone so that bodies could be thrown into it without delay, when the churchyard was no longer sufficient. Additional killing by fire and by water are thus considered two good measures after staking to ensure the end of vampirism.

But who should be the killer? It is said that the killer should be motivated, since a person seeking revenge is more likely to sustain the terror and fright until death is finally accomplished. A vampire who has only been half-killed because the killer has run away in panic is a thousand times more dangerous than an ordinary vampire. Countless men, whose fiances were bled to death by the evil creatures, form the main corpus of vampire hunters and killers.

The victim must smear the bites on her neck with the
blood that has issued from the dead body, as it is really
her own blood flowing in someone else's veins and this
act is the only cure to heal the bites.

Sometimes, however, it is the victim who gathers enough courage to kill the
beast who is slowly but surely sucking her life. After the killing is over, the
victim must smear the bites on her neck with the blood that has issued from
the dead body, as it is really her own blood flowing in someone else's veins
and this act is the only cure to heal the bites.

Epilogue

We have come to the end of our journey through the word of myth, legend, true facts and stories of vampires. Our fascination with these creatures of darkness, who enter our world at the twilight of time, space, spiritual boundaries, and the thin line between love and death, is seemingly never-ending. Vampires are with us always, and my own sense is that they will always be.

The enormous worldwide success of author Stephenie Meyer's *Twilight* book series, now also in film, testifies to the hypnotic quality vampires hold over millions of readers, who are plunged into the abyss where the supernatural merges with the human world as they read about the romantic struggles of Bella and Edward.

Vampires have been portrayed as arch seducers in the film *Bram Stoker's Dracula*, based on the original 1897 novel, as melancholic aristocrats in *Interview with the Vampire*, drawn from Anne Rice's novel, as rock stars in *Queen of the Damned*, as the frightening pale undead in *Nosferatu*, the German silent classic that is perhaps one of the most disquieting screen adaptations of vampires, and as creatures of the twilight in Werner Herzog's classic *Nosferatu the Vampire*. Online, there are endless websites with vampire facts, images, anecdotes and stories. As stated at the beginning of our book, vampires are not a local phenomenon, but they are everywhere and have always existed in all cultures. They live successfully in books, on the screen, on the Internet, even in popular TV series such as *Buffy, The Vampire Slayer*. We can be sure they live in

Sarah Michelle Gellar is Buffy
Summers in the popular TV series
Buffy, The Vampire Slayer.

our real world too, not just in the media, but in woods, small villages, underground beneath our cities, at the edges of society, but firmly there.

In our exploration we have seen that vampires live in the shadows of our world, and we must consider that they live in the shadows of our psyche too. Their erotic bloodsucking, their seduction from love into death, their refusal to peacefully depart after death into the next world, are all familiar behaviours we encounter in relationships focused on power struggles, dependence, dominance, and the holding on emotionally and psychically to a relationship long after it has died. Often these psychological tendencies occur as a result of unbearable emotional pain, when a person has experienced a deeply traumatic event from which he or she has never healed. An 'inner vampire' then appears in dreams, in daydreams, in fears, in one's relationship with oneself and with others: the personality becomes possessed by the inner vampire that tragically tears apart the psyche, never letting go. The only path to healing is through ancient wisdom, which acknowledges the existence of the inner vampire and also knows how to kill it by piercing its heart with a cross, the symbol of faith. It is indeed faith and self-care that protect us from these demonic creatures' clutches. The possessive spirits will try to resist, as we have seen throughout the book, but it is possible to overcome them with enough determination and a great sense of optimism in the face of darkness.

Vampires do exist and are everywhere, and we will always fall victim to them and what they represent. As seductive as they are, we must recognize them as creatures of the shadows. Denial of their presence in our lives is what humans have attempted for centuries, as this book chronicles.

Listen to the shadows, catch a glimpse of movement from the corner of your eye, watch the shapes change steathily in the darkness: they are all there. Protect yourself and know this is an ancient struggle, waged from time immemorial, between man and vampire.